The book of
Reptiles
R A Lanworn

HAMLYN
London · New York · Sydney · Toronto

Published by
THE HAMLYN PUBLISHING GROUP LIMITED
London · New York · Sydney · Toronto
Hamlyn House, Feltham, Middlesex, England
Copyright © The Hamlyn Publishing Group Limited 1972

ISBN 0 600 31273 9

Printed in Spain.
by Printer, Industria Grafica, S.A. Tuset 19,
Barcelona, San Vicente dels Horts, 1972
Deposito Legal B. 9553–1972
Mohn Gordon Ltd, London

The book of
Reptiles

Contents

Reptiles and Man

About 150 million years ago the Earth was dominated by the reptiles. There were sixteen main groups, including giant dinosaurs that lumbered across the land on their hind legs, pterodactyls that glided over the water in search of fishes and long-necked plesiosaurs that wallowed in the swamps. As time passed this Golden Age of Reptiles waned in the path of the ascendancy of the mammals. The first mammals had diverged from a primitive reptile stock prior to the rise of the dinosaurs and their contemporaries. The birds developed from a branch of the dinosaurs and continued to evolve after the decline of the reptiles.

Today there remain only four major groups of reptiles, the turtles, the crocodilians, the little-known Tuatara and the lizards and snakes. All these creatures have in common certain features which are characteristic of the reptile group. They all have a dry, scaly skin, and are able to breathe in air. They produce shelled eggs and their body temperature is dependent on external conditions.

It is evident from many of the mythologies and religions of the world that reptiles have had a profound impact on man. The snake or serpent is referred to constantly. To ancient man the serpent became a symbol of wisdom, fertility and the power of God.

The Greeks, in particular, attributed wisdom to the serpent. This is shown by the serpent's association with oracles in Greek mythology; for example, Apollo's oracle at Delphi was the sanctuary of a python before Apollo slew it.

An indication of the deep-rooted association of the snake with fertility is given when a parallel is drawn between a legend of the Hebrews, as outlined in Genesis, and a legend of the Ashanti people of Ghana. In both cases it was the serpent which imparted the secret of life, the secret of procreation, to Man and Woman. In the case of the Ashanti legend the message-bearer was a python and today the python is revered by members of a python clan. In contrast, the Hebrew

Previous page   The spines of the Iguana add to its grotesque appearance.

The temptation and the expulsion of Adam and Eve from the Garden of Eden, as depicted by Michelangelo in the Sistine Chapel at the Vatican.

serpent was condemned for imparting this knowledge and thus tempting Eve so that she and Adam were expelled from the Garden of Eden. Consequently the serpent in Judeo-Christian tradition has become a symbol of evil.

This is strange when one considers that the serpent was used as a sign of the power of God by Moses when his staff was transformed into a serpent before the eyes of Pharaoh. Perhaps the serpent's role in the temptation was designed, by the authors of Genesis, to crush old beliefs and prevent the worshipping of any god other than the God of Abraham.

The serpent is closely associated with many religions. According to one of the Hindu myths of creation, the prelude to the creation involved the great serpent Ananta, a cobra with many heads, floating on the waters of Nara and bearing the sleeping god Vishnu. Ananta was the king of the Nagas, who were the children of the mother serpent, Kadru.

Another Naga king is featured in Buddhist mythology. While Siddhartha, later to become Buddha, sought enlightenment under a tree, the forces of evil tried to tempt him from his purpose. However, Siddhartha resisted and on the twenty-eighth day obtained enlightenment, and became the Buddha. Having failed, the evil forces withdrew but evoked a violent storm, while Buddha remained deep in thought beneath the tree. The compassionate Naga king, Mucilinda, coiled himself beneath Buddha, lifting him off the soaking earth, and then he spread his seven heads above Buddha to keep him dry until the storm had ceased.

The favourite god of ancient Mexico and Central America was Quetzalcoatl, the Plumed Serpent. This deity was a compound of the beautiful Quetzal, a bird found in the rainforest of southern Mexico, and the rattlesnake. It is well represented in ancient architecture found throughout most of southern Mexico, Yucatan and Guatemala.

In this late seventeenth century Rajasthani painting the Hindu god Vishnu is reclining on the many-headed serpent, Ananta, which is floating on the waters of Nara. Vishnu is resting between two periods of cosmic evolution: the old world has been destroyed and the new one has not yet been created.

Turtles feature widely in mythology and religion. In Hindu tradition the second incarnation of the god Vishnu takes the form of a turtle, Kurma. The turtle also plays an important role in the mythology of the North American Indian. For example, a creation legend of the woodland Indians (the Iroquois, Hurons and Wyandots) involves the Great Turtle and Little Turtle. A little magical earth brought forth from the great waters and placed on the back of the Great Turtle grew to form the land, supported all the while by the Turtle. But the land was cloaked in darkness. So the Great Turtle asked Little Turtle to make a light in the sky. Little Turtle climbed up into the heavens and was carried round the sky in a cloud, collecting lightning. She made two bright balls of it in the sky, one large and one small, the Sun and the Moon. Then the Great Turtle ordered the burrowing animals to make holes in the corners of the sky so that the Sun and Moon could descend through one and ascend through the other as they circled the sky. So there was day and night.

The crocodile too has been deified. It was worshipped for example by the ancient Egyptians. Sebek was the chief crocodile deity. Initially, he was a rather insignificant water-god of the city of Crocodilopolis in Faiyum, but with the coming of the Twelfth Dynasty he became the god of the Pharaohs and was worshipped all over the land. Consequently, the most sacred crocodile kept in ancient Egypt was the one in which Sebek manifested himself. It was kept in Lake Moeris in Faiyum and priests decorated its front legs and its ears with gold and precious stones. Choice food was fed to it by pilgrims. The great veneration felt by the ancient Egyptians for the crocodile is clearly shown by the fact that it was considered a supreme honour to fall into the Nile and be eaten by one. In addition, Herodotus reported that each household possessed its tame crocodile, which was well looked after and upon death embalmed and placed in a sacred tomb. In fact crocodile mummies have been discovered in recent excavations of ancient tombs. To this day, in Pakistan, fakirs keep sacred crocodiles, which are often fed on goats, bought by devout pilgrims.

In view of this deification of certain reptiles, it is rather strange that Western man today regards many reptiles with fear and revulsion. So often they are animals to be avoided or killed on sight, even when harmless.

There are undoubtedly very good reasons why man should dislike and fear certain reptiles. Encounters with

The Anaconda's highly polished scales, like those of all snakes, reflect the light and the resultant glistening appearance of the body gives rise to the common misconception that snakes have wet or unpleasantly slimy skins. In fact, the skin of the snake, and indeed all other reptiles, is quite dry.

crocodiles and venomous snakes are likely to have fatal consequences. However, a non-venomous snake often arouses just as much fear as a venomous one, even though it is known to be harmless. Man's revulsion is thus frequently based on something other than a logical sense of danger.

It has been suggested that our antipathy for snakes is inherited from our ancestors, who walked barefoot and not unnaturally dreaded treading upon a snake which could inflict a fatal bite. This would not, however, explain the dislike of the harmless lizards.

Perhaps man's antipathy to reptiles lies in their appearance. Most reptiles appear devoid of those features which inspire our affection in other animals. In contrast to the warm texture of soft fur or feathers, the dry, scaly reptile skin leaves an impression of hardness and armour and, in the case of snakes, the smooth and often glistening appearance of the body gives rise to the popular misconception of unpleasant sliminess. Many lizards are adorned with spines and frills and are garish in colour, all of which gives them an exceedingly grotesque appearance.

Mammals, in particular, have behaviour patterns which make it easy for us to credit them with the possession of human qualities, such as affection and playfulness. It would be difficult indeed to credit a reptile with such attributes. Many mammals appear to exhibit human emotions such as contentment or anger, while reptiles fail to display any sign of such feelings.

The movements of reptiles are often alarming. The snake slithers mysteriously along without visible means of propulsion, while lizards make sudden darting and thrusting movements of head and body. The constant flicking of the long, forked tongue of the snake undoubtedly enhances its sinister appearance.

Equally disturbing is the manner in which some reptiles maintain a death-like stillness for long periods of time, while the snake, lacking eyelids, has a cold, fixed stare which can be rather unnerving.

The fact that some reptiles inhabit dark corners, inaccessible to man, may also add to the aura of mystery and evil surrounding them.

Many of the factors which have helped to bring about this dislike of reptiles are based on misconception and ignorance. It has already been mentioned that it is quite commonly thought that snakes have a slimy skin. In fact, reptiles in general are thought to be cold, wet and slimy by many people. How incorrect this is. Reptiles are certainly cold-blooded animals. Scientists call this condition *poikilothermal*, which means that the body temperature is largely dependent on the temperature of the immediate surroundings, and is not maintained internally as in birds and mammals. Except for a few temperate reptiles which can live in cool parts, the greatest number of reptiles are tropical or subtropical and need warmth to survive, and so, in fact, they feel pleasantly warm to the touch. The skins

Man's fear of the Nile and other crocodiles is justified in that encounters with them could prove fatal. However, it is usually only large old specimens, confined in small pools, which are naturally belligerent.

of many lizards and snakes have highly polished scales which reflect the light, and give the appearance of being wet and perhaps even slimy, but they are quite dry, unless the animals have just left the vicinity of water. Even then the water rolls from them as their skin is nearly waterproof, and so they do not remain wet for very long.

Snakes are often reputed to possess hypnotic powers enabling them to render their victims motionless and so easily overpower and finally swallow them. There is no truth whatever in this suggestion. Certain wild

animals including some of the rodents become 'rooted to the ground' when exposed to danger and other conditions. The scientist calls this 'freezing'. It is therefore conceivable that, when a snake has been observed intent on capturing an immobile rodent, instead of this rodent being under the snake's hypnotic powers, it was probably freezing or it might have already been bitten by the snake, prior to being swallowed.

Charges of ferocity and aggressiveness are frequently made against these much maligned creatures and yet very few merit such accusations. Large, old crocodiles and alligators confined in small pools will attack their own kind, or any other intruders. They appear to prefer a solitary existence, but by and large very few indeed are naturally belligerent.

Any wild animal in restricted quarters, with no escape route, is likely to attack. It is simply a matter of survival and cannot truthfully be described as aggression. Reptiles react in just such a manner if they are cornered, but given the chance to escape to some undergrowth or perhaps a hole in the ground nearby, they will invariably do so.

The King Cobra (*Naja hannah*) has always been acclaimed as the world's most dangerous and aggressive snake, but I consider this reputation to be ill deserved. They are certainly snakes to be reckoned with, for they are the world's largest venomous snakes, growing up to 18 feet (5.5 metres) in length. They are also equipped with huge poison fangs and very large capacity glands, containing their highly potent venom. Anyone bitten would be exceedingly lucky to survive, and even very large animals have died within minutes

of being bitten. However, these snakes do not readily attack; they much prefer to escape.

On one occasion when I met King Cobras in open country I unwittingly approached to within 20 feet (6 metres) of them. On sighting me they reared up and expanded their hoods in a most threatening manner, and then they kept their heads pointing towards me while they gently swayed. I had kept these species of snakes in captivity, but this was my first encounter in open scrub. I halted and waited in rather a dilemma, but after a very short time I ceased to be worried. Their hoods gradually became smaller, their heads were lowered from about 3 feet (1 metre) to ground level and they gently slithered away to a less frequented clearing. They had had every opportunity to attack me but did not do so. The King Cobra is a cannibal snake, feeding entirely on other snakes and large lizards. It is therefore difficult to feed in captivity, but, if it is possible to supply it with the right food, it will adapt to its captivity remarkably quickly and become quite docile.

The mambas (*Dendroaspis* species) of Africa are extremely venomous snakes but my late friend C. J. P. Ionides, who captured more mambas and other African poisonous snakes than anyone else, had never known one attack if it could escape instead. He also maintained that the large vipers, the Puff Adder (*Bitis arietans*) and the Gaboon Viper (*Bitis gabonica*), were just too lazy to move away and only attacked if nearly trodden upon. So all snakes cannot be accused of aggression and in fact very few attack without provocation.

Often snakes are credited with the ability to travel at phenomenal speeds and fiction writers even use expressions such as 'fast as galloping horses', or 'fast as

The Black Mamba (Dendroaspis polylepis) and the other mambas of Africa are extremely venomous snakes. Fortunately they usually attack only when escape is impossible.

express trains'. Experiments with reptiles have proved such descriptions to be quite false. Maximum speeds, and these only attained for short distances, have been found to be about 10 miles (16 kilometres) per hour. The majority of snakes travel at less than half this speed, which is about the speed we travel when walking quickly. For animals without limbs (excepting the few snakes with vestigial limbs which are in no way helpful for locomotion) they are very agile creatures, particularly when travelling in undergrowth which would retard other animals; but they are in no way the lightning creatures so often described.

All over the world a variety of stories have evolved about reptiles, particularly snakes. Although these have no basis in fact, they do serve to maintain man's fear, and hence dislike, of snakes. The folklore of the North American Indian is responsible for the 'Hoop Snake' story, which is still believed in some outlying country districts. Some of the oldest inhabitants explain that in very hilly country, the 'Hoop Snake', a supposedly fierce venomous snake, chases its victims by the simple expedient of forming a hoop with its body, tail in mouth, and bowling after them at unbelievable speeds. Even this story was surpassed by one told by the old mountain people in the regions of the southern Appalachian Mountains. It concerned the Coachwhip Snake (*Masticophis flagellum*), which is fairly common in the area. This snake was reputed not only to chase its quarry but, after capture, to twine itself around the victim and a tree, and then to proceed to whip the helpless victim to death with its tail.

Another example of man's ignorance and even stupidity causing or enhancing his dislike for the snake comes from the United States. The Milk Snake (*Lampropeltis doliata*) is often accused of stealing milk, and in farming districts it is slaughtered mercilessly, especially when seen near barns where it hunts for the small rodents upon which it lives. It is an attractively coloured snake with rings and blotches of scarlet, black and white. It is extremely docile, but because it is often seen near cow-barns its behaviour is misinterpreted. Even a little thought on the subject should have absolved it from blame. No cow would ever permit a snake with rows of needle-like teeth to suckle from her and secondly snakes dislike milk and will refuse to drink it.

In South Africa the Cape Cobra (*Naja capensis*) was often accused of milking cattle and witnesses to the feat were able to describe the act in the local papers! For anatomical reasons no snake can suckle, and so all these reports are without foundation.

Of course it is not only reports of the drinking habits of snakes which are suspect; their eating habits are often grossly exaggerated. All their food is swallowed whole for, although they have very many teeth, these are needle-like and are only used to hold the food and assist in passing it into the throat. The neck distends, and the jaws dislocate, allowing the complete animal or bird to be swallowed. The largest of the snakes, the pythons, the Anaconda (*Eunectes murinus*), and the Boa Constrictor (*Constrictor constrictor*), may swallow small deer, goats or wild boars.

In South Africa it has often been reported that the Cape Cobra has been seen milking cattle. Such reports are completely without foundation.

However, it is only the largest adults of these species that are capable of such enormous meals. The smaller specimens feed on rodents, small piglets and birds. Even the largest specimens would have difficulty in eating a human, although there are a few authenticated reports of such incidents, one of which took place in the Philippine Islands a few years ago. There is certainly no truth in the allegations that the large snakes swallow bullocks. Even the Boa Constrictor in Swiss Family Robinson would have been incapable of swallowing the family's donkey!

The forked or bifurcated tongue of snakes seems to be a major visual factor in instilling fear into the beholder and often it is incorrectly referred to as a sting. This very fine sensory organ is in fact harmless. Its method of flicking in and out is quite fascinating to watch, and in some species in which the tips of the fork are brightly coloured it is used as a decoy for the capture of small lizards. To some people it appears to be so much like a 'sting' that I have had snakes brought to me which had had their tongues snipped off with scissors to render them harmless. One particular snake was a venomous species and it was only due to its docility that its captor had not been seriously bitten.

On another occasion when an albino Indian Cobra was brought to me I was informed by its owner that it was quite safe to handle as he had had the fangs removed in India before he brought it to this country. No doubt it had had its fangs removed, but I discovered that this had taken place several months earlier and in the meantime a very fine pair of new ones had grown. It was fortunate indeed that this snake had become tame, as it had not only been freely handled by its owner, but also by his young daughters, and on at least one occasion in a very crowded London club.

The teeth of snakes, including the poison fangs, are in fact regularly discarded and replaced, and so even a very old snake has a good set of teeth.

As well as fearing or deifying snakes man is sometimes fascinated or mystified by them. Pipe music and swaying serpents have been associated from ancient times in Asiatic countries, and it is not surprising that the colourful exhibition of snake charming fascinates Europeans who visit the Near and Far East. Some tourists are probably more attracted by the display of showmanship than by the snakes taking part. Usually these displays take place in a corner of a town square or in one of the North African casbahs. The instrumentalist sits cross-legged playing whining 'music' on a pipe which consists of a hollow gourd and short lengths of bamboo welded together with beeswax. At least, the old pipes were made in this way. The last ones I inspected were modernized with plastic resins. The cobras rear up with expanded heads and sway slightly from side to side. What is so surprising about the whole exhibition is the fact that the snakes do not hear the music, for they are deaf to these whining sounds! Certainly it appears that the snakes 'sit' up and sway, but cobras will invariably raise their heads, extend their hoods and sway whenever disturbed. If something is waved slowly in front of them, they will follow it about by swaying their heads, but the music is completely unnecessary. I have replaced the gourd pipe with pieces of cloth, rubber balls, and other articles, and managed to produce the same effect; and on one occasion to prove the point I waved a banana in front of the snake and produced even more satisfactory rhythmic swaying! In 1955 I demonstrated, on television, this snake charming without music, using a cobra. For safety I attached a belt halfway down the cobra and fastened it to the base of the basket, but when the cameras were recording some very fine swaying of the snake we noticed that it extended further and further from the basket in a most spectacular manner. This was rather puzzling until we discovered that the snake had shed its skin from midway, where its belt had been placed, and simply crawled out leaving belt and slough behind! We had demonstrated our point regarding 'music' and snakes and it had emphasized how careful one must be in handling dangerous snakes. We should have checked our snake more thoroughly.

Until recently I had always accepted that the charming of snakes was the monopoly of the orientals but two rather amusing stories have come to my attention in which rattlesnakes have been charmed instrumentally in the western United States. The first is mentioned in Lawrence Klauber's large work on rattlesnakes. It is

A snake charmer with an Indian Cobra (Naja naja) and mongoose, in Madras. The snake is responding to the movement of the pipe and not to the music.

about a fruit picker who played a harmonica to them, but the second story, which I subsequently discovered in an old scientific book of 1870 by Louis Figuier, is a report which is so farcical that I feel it should be given as written. It commences 'Rattlesnakes are revered by some of the American natives, who know how to lure them from their houses without killing them; for it is a singular fact that this terrible animal is not insensible to the sound of music. Chateaubriand's remarks will be read with interest, "In the month of July 1791", says the celebrated writer, "we were travelling—with some savage families of the Ounoutagnes. One day when we stopped in a plain on the banks of the river Genedie, a rattlesnake entered our camp. We had a Canadian amongst us who played on a flute; wishing to amuse us, he approached the animal with this new kind of weapon. At the approach of his enemy, the splendid reptile at once coiled itself up spirally, flattened its head, puffed out its cheeks, contracted its ears, and showed its envenomed fangs, whilst its forked tongue moved rapidly, and its eyes burned like red-hot coals; its body became inflated with rage, rose and fell like a pair of bellows; its dilated skin bristled with scales; and its tail, which produced a sinister sound oscillated with lightning rapidity. Now the Canadian began to play his flute. The Snake made a movement expressive of surprise, gradually drew its head backwards, closed its inflamed mouth, and, as the musical sounds struck it, the eyes lost their sharpness, the vibration of its tail relaxed, and the noise which it made became weaker, and finally died away altogether; the coiled-up line became less perpendicular, the orbs of the changed Snake opened, and in their turn rested in wider concentric circles on the ground. The scales of the skin were also lowered, and immediately recovered their wonted brilliancy, and turning its head slowly towards the musician, it remained immovable in an attitude of pleased attention. At this moment the Canadian walked away a few steps, drawing low and monotonous tones from his flute; the reptile lowered its neck, opened a way among the fine grass with its head, and crawled in the steps of the musician who thus fascinated him, stopping when he stopped, and following him when he began to move away. The snake was thus conducted from our camp in the midst of a throng of spectators, as many Red Skins as Europeans—who could hardly believe their eyes".'

This scientific report does at least show the great progress that has been made in the study of natural history during recent years, and it is gratifying to know that we are learning about the animals whose lives were previously a complete mystery. Television, travel, and natural history documentaries have increased the thirst for information and, in conjunction with the publishing world, fostered a much more reasoned understanding of the maligned reptiles.

Left According to a legend which originated in the region of the southern Appalachian Mountains, the Coachwhip Snake not only chases its prey but whips it to death with its tail, after pinning it to a tree with its coils.

Below left The snake's forked tongue, well displayed by this Grass Snake, seems to be a major visual factor in instilling fear into the beholder, and often it is incorrectly referred to as a sting. This sensory organ is in fact quite harmless.

Below An African Python (Python sebae) swallowing a white rat. The smaller constricting snakes feed on rodents, piglets or birds, while the larger specimens can swallow small deer, goats or wild boars. There is no truth in the assertions that snakes can swallow animals as large as bullocks.

The Golden Age of Reptiles

The very earliest reptiles evolved from the amphibious creatures which lived on the earth over 200 million years ago. They inhabited large tracts of swamp and were more characteristic of amphibians than modern reptiles. Scientists have thus experienced difficulty in deciding whether the fossilized remains are reptilian or amphibian, so intermediate are they. One of the lines of demarcation resulted from the advent of the reptilian egg, which is laid on land. The amphibians lay their eggs in water, and fertilization is external.

The very first of the reptiles are known as cotylosaurs or stem reptiles, and it is from these that the whole, great, varied family of primitive and modern reptiles has evolved. They were heavy, short-legged and cumbersome creatures, with an appearance somewhat similar to corpulent crocodiles! By the time that the true reptiles had become fairly widespread over the Earth, their earliest ancestors had disappeared, leaving only their fossilized remains lying in what were the great swamps.

Many of the groups evolved into increasingly terrestrial creatures, becoming slimmer and much more agile, and others developed a form of walking and running involving only their hind limbs. Over the millions of years, the forelimbs became very small and nearly useless in certain of these groups of reptiles. Changes in diet also occurred, with many groups becoming increasingly carnivorous, and others developing as herbivores.

The dinosaurs formed one of the largest groups of primitive reptiles. It was a group containing creatures of a tremendous range of shape and size. To most people the name 'dinosaur' conjures up an image of an enormous lizard-like animal; but the word, which was invented by Richard Owen about 120 years ago, was intended as a collective name for a whole group of primitive reptiles. The smallest of the group were the size of a domestic hen and the largest were 80 feet (24 metres) long and weighed many tons. It was in the

Previous page   Triceratops, a reptile from the past.

Tyrannosaurus was a huge flesh-eating dinosaur. All its weight was carried on its heavy hind limbs.

Mesozoic Era, the Reptile Age, that the reptiles completely overran the Earth. This era began over 200 million years ago and lasted for about 150 million years which, when considered in relation to man's existence of about 20,000 years, is difficult even to contemplate. During the Mesozoic Era, some of the primitive terrestrial creatures returned to the swamps and once more took up an aquatic way of life. Others evolved very light bones and became the flying creatures so often depicted in the illustrations of prehistoric times, the pterodactyls with their bat-like wings. Many of the flying reptiles were fish-eaters. Their membranous wings allowed them to fly and drift aloft for a considerable period and it is thought that they caught their fishes by swooping just above the sea, as many of our present-day seabirds do.

Some of the earliest types of dinosaur were the

coelurosaurs, slightly built, bird-like theropods, which used only their hind limbs for walking. Their forelimbs were exceedingly short and had developed 'hands' suitable for holding their prey. Their most bird-like relative was the 'Ostrich Dinosaur' (*Struthiomimus*), which in shape and size was very much like its namesake. Some very fine fossil remains of them have been found, showing that their 'hands' were equipped with opposable fingers very much like those of present-day chameleons.

Descended from this same theropod line were the largest flesh-eating creatures to have appeared on the Earth: the Tyrant Dinosaur (*Tyrannosaurus*) is an example. They were 50 feet (15 metres) in length and weighed many tons, but their forelegs were very small and appear, from their skeletons, to have been of no use to them. All their weight had to be carried on their two heavily built rear limbs. Their jaws were tremendous, opening widely enough to grasp the large herbivorous dinosaurs which they tore to pieces with their curved teeth.

Many of the herbivorous dinosaurs were even larger

Stegosaurus was a giant herbivorous dinosaur with large, erect, bony plates along its back and spikes on its tail. It is thought that this armour helped to protect Stegosaurus from the aggressive carnivorous dinosaurs.

and heavier than the Tyrant Dinosaurs; but the sauropods, as they are named, needed four legs to support their great bulk. *Brontosaurus* and *Diplodocus* both grew to 80 feet (24 metres) in length and it is estimated that they weighed up to 30 tons or more. *Brachiosaurus*, which had less tail but more bulk than the previous two, is thought to have weighed about 50 tons. These creatures spent all their lives in the swamps and would probably have found travelling on land without the help of the buoyancy of water very difficult, in much the same way as the hippopotamus does today. Their food, the lush vegetation growing profusely in the swamps, was also close at hand.

It is remarkable how some dinosaur names have captured the attention of the public. I have found, for instance, that many people know the name *Iguanodon* without knowing anything about the creature. Remains of this dinosaur of the ornithischian group (the dinosaurs just described all belong to the saurischian group) were discovered in Kent and there was much publicity at the time. It was a huge, 25 foot (7.5 metre) 'dragon', which walked nearly upright. There were some dinosaurs belonging to this group which were more striking to look at. For example, *Stegosaurus* was a 25 foot (7.5 metre) giant, which had 3 feet (1 metre) high bony plates erected along the back, and spikes on the tail, and *Triceratops* had horns on its head and a great flange of spikes around its neck. Such pieces of armour helped to protect these herbivores from the aggressive carnivorous dinosaurs.

The pterodactyls or flying reptiles were as bizarre as the terrestrial ones and, although many of them were quite small, there were some giants, such as *Pteranodon* which had a wingspan of 20 feet (6 metres) or more. The largest fossil specimens of flying reptiles were discovered in Kansas. The wingspan was 25 feet (7.5 metres).

By the end of the Mesozoic Era, the dinosaurs were no more. It is interesting to contemplate the consequences had they not become extinct, but remained on the Earth. It is true that they lasted longer than any other group, but their disappearance is puzzling to scientists. They have had to sift the story from the earth, digging and delving in all parts of the world for

Above left Brontosaurus was a gigantic herbivore which, it is thought, spent its life in the swamps, where the buoyancy of water would have helped to support its great bulk.

Left Diplodocus was a herbivore which was very similar to Brontosaurus.

Above right Iguanodon was a huge herbivorous dinosaur which walked nearly upright on its hind limbs.

Right Pterodactyls or flying reptiles were as bizarre as the terrestrial forms.

fossilized remains and fitting lots of little pieces into a gigantic jig-saw. Even fossil eggs have been discovered and during one very famous excavation in Mongolia many years ago, a dinosaur's nest with eggs was unearthed. It contained the crushed skull of a smaller lizard which was apparently caught stealing one of the eggs. Millions of years later, a similar situation occurs today, when the monitor lizard raids the crocodile's nest and gets caught.

Why did the dinosaurs disappear from the face of the Earth? No one knows for certain. In all probability, the effect of the Earth becoming cooler changed the whole pattern of life, as did the drying up of the swamps and the development of hardwood forests.

Left Triceratops was a herbivorous dinosaur which had impressive horns on its head and a great flange around its neck. These appendages, like those of Stegosaurus, would have provided some protection from the attacks of the carnivorous dinosaurs.

Above The Tuatara of New Zealand looks rather like a lizard. However it is the sole survivor of a group of very ancient reptiles which flourished long before the rise of the great dinosaurs. This unique creature is therefore frequently described as a living fossil.

The herbivorous dinosaurs lost their main source of food and gradually died out, and the carnivorous groups automatically followed suit. In addition, the dinosaurs most probably suffered from competition with the more adaptable mammal group that was rapidly expanding. The reptiles had the disadvantage of an exceedingly small brain relative to their body size, while the mammals had the advantage of a large brain. It is thought that, as well as depriving the dinosaurs of their food, mammals also devoured their huge eggs.

Whatever the reasons, the Golden Age of Reptiles ended and the bird and mammal era commenced. Only those reptiles which were able to adapt to the changing environment survived. The crocodilians, turtles, and the Tuatara of today have changed little from those ancestors which survived the fall of the reptiles, while the lizards and snakes have become extensively modified. Whatever the form modern reptiles assume, we know that they developed from that ancient group of stem reptiles, the Cotylosauria.

To go along to the museums and see the reconstructed dinosaur skeletons found in far off countries is fascinating but, for real excitement, one must watch the palaeontologist unearthing the remains of creatures who roamed the Earth millions of years ago.

The great volcanic eruptions on the Earth have been instrumental in exposing these giants from the past.

Above It is fascinating to watch the palaeontologist at work, unearthing the remains of extinct creatures, such as this plesiosaur, which inhabited the Earth millions of years ago.

Right The rare Komodo Dragon is the largest lizard to be found in the world today.

Their remains were buried miles deep, but faults and fissures in the Earth's crust have brought them nearer to the surface. The manner in which these fossil remains have been discovered often provides a fascinating story. One I found especially intriguing comes from Wyoming, where a veritable mine of prehistoric reptiles was found by a New York scientist, Dr Granger, when he was visiting an old shepherds' shelter. He noticed that some of the pieces of stone, with which the hut had been constructed, were fossilized bone, and had been quarried locally. When a subsequent search took place, the whole area proved to be a veritable 'cemetery' of the remains of dinosaurs and other primitive creatures. It eventually became famous among the world's scientists and gained the name of Bone Cabin Quarry. It was from here that the first complete skeleton of *Brontosaurus* was unearthed, and this find certainly captured the public's imagination. Now it was not only the palaeontologists who wished to dig for bones, but others from all walks of life. For many it was for the pleasure of finding something from the past, but when the wealthy museums offered fabulous rewards for complete skeletons, a rush to gather bones commenced, and a type of market evolved where fossil bones went to the highest bidder.

The unearthing of the more or less complete *Brontosaurus* occupied a team of experts for nearly a year; and the searching for missing bones, the assembling and erecting and, finally, the placing in the huge hall of the American Natural History Museum took nearly five years of dedicated work. It was a triumphant achievement in that it was the first time that a full sized *Brontosaurus* had ever been exhibited. It is 67 feet (20 metres) in length and 15 feet (5 metres) in height. The weight of this specimen when alive was estimated at 80 tons, making it one of the heaviest creatures which ever roamed the Earth. When the bones of *Iguanodon* were first found in Britain about 150 years ago, the scientist who discovered them estimated that they were from a creature 200 feet (61 metres) long! This length was proved to be an exaggeration a few years later when some Belgian coal miners unexpectedly came upon a complete skeleton of *Iguanodon* in a fracture of the rocks. When this was reconstructed and the bones compared with those of the earlier one found in Britain, it was agreed that 30 feet (9 metres) would have been a more accurate estimate.

In the world today we have about 6,000 species of reptiles, belonging to four Orders or groups, very many less than when the reptiles were in the ascendancy of their era and there were sixteen great Orders. Three of the present day Orders have changed little over the millions of years, except in numbers of species and in size. The Order Chelonia comprises about 200 species of tortoises, terrapins and turtles, and although there are some wonderful variations among them, a few are not greatly removed from *Triassochelys*, which lived in the Triassic period, 180 to 150 million years ago. The same may be said of the Order Crocodilia which now only contains twenty-three species of crocodile, alligator and caiman. Many of these have similarities with *Protosuchus* which lived in the swamps in the Triassic period. The Order Rhynchocephalia is only represented by one species, that unique lizard-like creature which is so very well protected in New Zealand, the Tuatara (*Sphenodon punctatus*). It has changed so very little from its early ancestors that it has earned the description 'living fossil'. The last Order is the Squamata which comprises the lizards and the snakes. It is among the members of the Order Squamata that there have been the greatest developments in shape and size. One of these changes has involved the loss of the limbs. At the present time there are about 3,000 species of lizards, ranging from tiny geckos of less than 1 inch (2.5 centimetres) to the large Komodo Dragon (*Varanus komodoensis*), which can be 10 feet (3 metres) in length. There are fewer species of snakes, about 2,700 in all. The worrying thought is that at present quite a number of species are dangerously close to extinction, in all the Orders except the Rhynchocephalia. That Order at least appears safe. It would be a great loss to the world if any of the modern reptiles disappeared as the dinosaurs have done, particularly if this happened through man's folly.

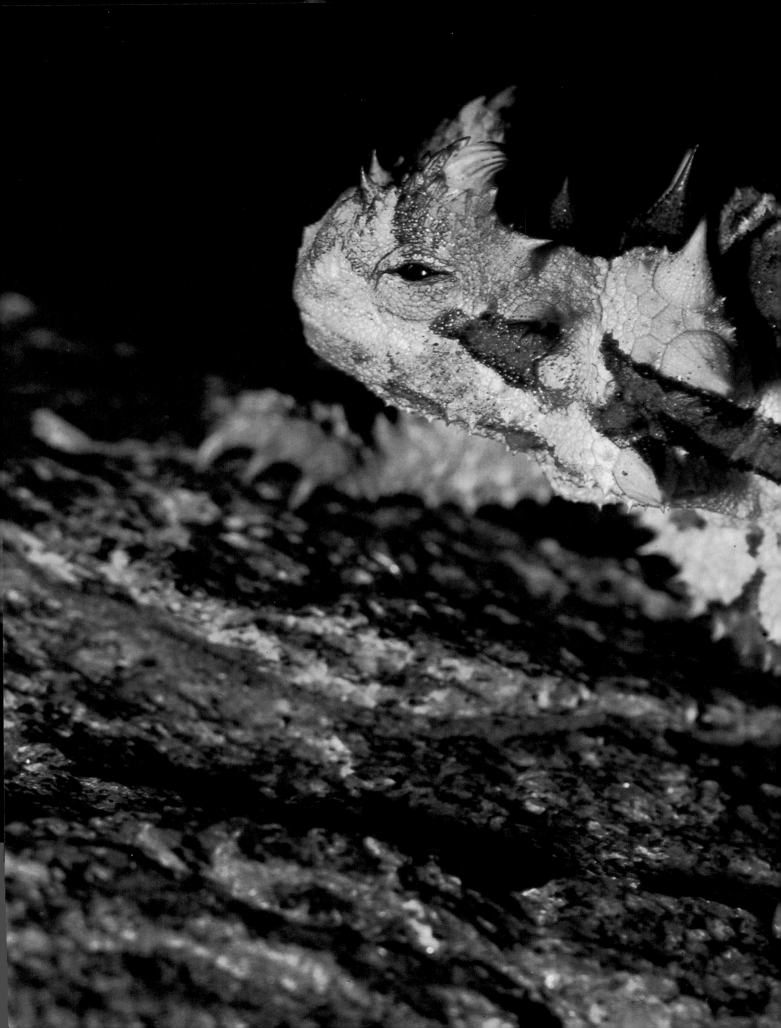

Ways of Life

If a little more were generally known about the lives of reptiles, it is certain that they would be more favourably looked upon, since in many ways they are unique. Some of their behaviour patterns and adaptations to a particular way of life are fascinating.

The way in which reptiles control their body temperature is unusual. They are cold-blooded, that is their body temperature cannot be controlled internally but is dependent on the environment. However, for each reptile species there is a range within which the body temperature must be maintained. This is achieved by the animal's behaviour.

Naturally one finds that tropical reptiles have a higher body temperature than specimens from cooler climates. The former spend much of their life in the sun, on the hot sun-heated rocks or sand, or perhaps on the top-most branches of trees. When the temperature they prefer is exceeded they then burrow under the surface of the ground or descend to lower, more shaded, branches. To increase their body temperature, many lizards flatten their body to present a larger surface area to the sun. To reduce heat absorption, they place their body at an angle to the sun so that the surface area presented to it is smaller. We find that some lizards, such as the agamas and the chameleons, can change colour to assist their temperature control, taking on a lightish hue to reflect excess heat.

Some reptiles will use pools of water to keep their temperature constant, or to reduce it. This form of control can often be observed in the reptile houses of zoos. It is not always possible to keep the air temperatures of small cages at the levels required by the inmates. Ideally the cages should be large enough to provide zones of temperature and surroundings, but this is not always practicable and so an average situation is arranged. In consequence, one can often see animals normally found away from water, such as the Gila Monster (*Heloderma suspectum*) of the Arizona desert, lying in the pools provided.

This same method of reducing body temperature was adopted by the Tuatara (*Sphenodon punctatus*) of New Zealand, at the London Zoo before a cooling system was devised. It was noticed that whenever the cage temperature reached about 16°C, which is cool for the majority of reptiles, the Tuatara would hurry into its burrow, or dive into its pool. Most other reptiles become torpid at low temperatures and can remain so for a considerable time without suffering damage, unless the temperature falls below 8°C or 10°C. However, a few degrees above the optimum temperature can prove dangerous. In several zoos

Previous page The fearsome-looking Australian Mountain Devil subsists on a very specialized diet of ants.

The Tuatara requires a lower environmental temperature than any other reptile.

32

where large crocodiles and alligators have been housed in glass-covered dens there have been cases of these animals dying of heat stroke, when the sun has raised the temperature just a few degrees. Reptiles which live in the world's hottest deserts are capable of thriving in a temperature of 40°C, but a rise of a few degrees above this is fatal.

A reptile's activity depends upon its body temperature and, unless this is within the preferred range, the animal will become inactive and will not attempt to feed. Many reptiles fast for long periods. Reptilian feeding habits are diverse. As to be expected, the herbivorous group, which includes only certain chelonians (tortoises, turtles and terrapins) and certain members of the iguanid family of lizards, will feed every day, in suitable conditions. Herbivores generally eat their leaves and fruit in the morning, have a siesta, and then feed again later in the day. The food is chopped up by the jaws until small enough to swallow. The carnivorous reptiles do not feed as frequently. They are opportunists which gorge when they have the chance to feed and fast, often for weeks or months, when food is not available.

For many reptiles, the diet changes as they grow to adult animals. The crocodilians when first hatched eat little and often. Their diet consists of small frogs, fishes and insects, which have to be a suitable size for swallowing, since most reptilian teeth are of no use for biting food into pieces. However, the crocodilians do have 'one up' on human dental replacement: during their life they may have more than forty replacement sets of teeth. Even so, they cannot bite off pieces of the larger animals upon which they feed when adult. Instead they have devised a method of feeding that has produced the many stories about 'crocodile larders'. These suggest that the carcasses of large animals, often severely mutilated, are placed in caves under overhanging river banks by crocodiles, to be eaten at a later date. In fact, the bodies have generally drifted to these resting places by accident, after the crocodilians have twisted and torn off their requirements. The large crocodilians kill their prey by dragging it under water or, if it is a fish, by crushing it in their powerful jaws. When given the opportunity, however, they are not averse to eating carrion found floating in the tropical rivers. This behaviour is made use of by the African trappers who hunt them for their skins. Large triple and quadruple barbed shark hooks are baited with pieces of meat, and left overnight at the water's edge to be swallowed by unsuspecting crocodilians. It is a very inhumane method of capture, but preferable to the manner in which they were often caught years ago in the upper reaches of the Orinoco River. I recently came upon an old report describing 'successful methods employed for catching the wary Alligator'. It reads 'live bait, for instance a dog with hooks attached to its back can be taken by canoe, and dropped in the water; it is seldom that the unfortunate cur is permitted to swim far before being seized. It is currently believed Alligators prefer dog flesh to all others.' The Alligators referred to are the Caiman, one species of which grows to more than 12 feet (4 metres) in length. There may be some foundation for the statement about dog flesh. Before the last war, Komodo Dragons (*Varanus komodoensis*), which were kept in a zoo at Surabaya, Indonesia, were fed largely on the town's pariah dogs. A well-travelled friend who visited the dragons at feeding time and watched them scuffle over their meal described the scene as the most horrible sight he had ever witnessed. Two of the first of these creatures to be seen in Europe were acquired by the London Zoo in 1927. How different was their feeding time. In a matter of months they became charming, docile giants, taking dead rats and pigeons from the hand and swallowing a dozen hens' eggs at one sitting, without cracking an egg. Probably on their own island of Sumba they took living creatures as food, but later one of these individuals, given the name of Sumbawa, had become trustworthy enough for small children to be able to sit upon its back. We had these two friendly giants for more than twelve years and hoped that they would breed, but we never obtained eggs from them. There was just a suspicion that they were attempting to be self-supporting by eating their own eggs. All the monitor lizards (the Komodo Dragons are the largest species) have an attraction for eggs and will raid not only the nests of birds, but also those of crocodiles and turtles, eating the eggs or the infants. This group of lizards is also valuable for the amount of rodents it eats. They hunt out rats very much as the terrier does and despatch them by vigorous shaking.

Many of the snakes are not so efficient in dealing with their prey. In many cases where fishes and amphibians form the major part of the diet, these are swallowed alive, the strong gastric juices causing their death afterwards. When snakes which have recently fed are handled roughly, they will often disgorge their food, and if the meal has been a frog or toad, it is not unusual to see the creature hop away. I had a Natterjack Toad for many years which was resurrected in this way from a Grass Snake!

The large constricting snakes, the pythons, the Boa Constrictor (*Constrictor constrictor*) and the Anaconda (*Eunectes murinus*), kill their prey by suffocation. They crush the victim and prevent it from breathing, but the bones are not broken as one would imagine. These snakes do not usually need to go hunting for their food. They more often lie coiled up in a well-camouflaged position waiting for a meal to come into reach. This

As well as eating mammals, the large Komodo Dragon will raid the nests of birds, turtles and crocodiles, and devour the eggs.

A Carpet Python feeding. The constricting snake kills its prey by crushing it with its coils and preventing it from breathing. When the victim ceases to struggle the snake swallows it head-first.

might consist of a wild pig, a small deer, a monkey or perhaps a large bird. They catch their prey by striking; throwing their head forward to gain a grip with their gaping jaws. At more or less the same time, they cast one or two coils, depending upon size, around the struggling animal. Every movement made by the victim causes the coils to become more taut. When struggling ceases the constrictor relaxes and, releasing the hold of its jaws, begins to search for the head. The flicking forked tongue seeks out every contour until its goal is reached, and then once more the gaping jaws grab the animal. It is rare for a snake to attempt to swallow its food other than head first. If it happens in captivity, the snake invariably releases its jaws, finds the 'right spot' and commences again. The swallowing process consists of the snake pushing its mouth over its food, and is assisted by four rows of teeth in the top jaw and two in the lower. They are needle-like teeth, slightly recurved towards the throat, and they take another grip every time the jaws are thrust forward. During the swallowing the jaws dislocate; each side of the lower jaw separates and moves independently, pulling the food towards the throat. A further action takes place to force the animal down the throat, starting as soon as it has been completely engulfed. The

constrictor forms a sharp bend with its body, just behind its head. By a slow rippling movement the meal is forced gradually along by the 'bend' travelling behind it. It sometimes takes several days for a snake to completely digest a large animal, and it is then that it is in a vulnerable condition and subject to attack by predators.

The venomous snakes are fortunate in that they can kill their prey more quickly, with little risk to themselves. The smaller, non-venomous snakes, on the other hand, are liable to be bitten by the rodents which they eat.

The venom of snakes is manufactured in highly developed salivary glands in the upper jaws, above the lips and behind the eyes. Broadly speaking, it mainly consists of two types, a neurotoxic or nerve poison and a haemotoxic or blood poison. In the elapine group of snakes, which contains the cobras, mambas and their relatives, the venom is mainly neurotoxic, and the bites produce nerve damage and paralysis. The viperine

A Night Adder (Causus rhombeatus) swallowing a toad. The needle-like teeth of snakes are incapable of a tearing action and so the prey is swallowed whole, the jaws dislocating in the process.

group of snakes mainly produces a haemotoxic venom. Within each group there are individual species which produce combinations of the two types of venom, which makes the study of snake venoms a very complex subject. A great deal of venom research is being conducted and scientists are now producing some very valuable life-saving drugs from these death-dealing venoms.

Snake venom is injected by means of two or more fangs which are set above the lips and behind the eyes in the snake's upper jaw. In the elapine group, the short fangs are fixed in the front of the jaw and the venom is chewed into the victim. Some of the cobras are able to 'spit' their venom in two fine sprays, which are usually aimed at the eyes of an intruder, in addition to giving a venomous bite. I have known both the Black-necked Cobra (*Naja nigricollis*) and the Ringhals (*Hemachatus haemachatus*) spray venom accurately on to the lens of goggles at a distance of more than 7 feet (2 metres). The viperine group of snakes have the

largest fangs, and these hypodermic-like teeth are hinged and are only erected when the mouth is fully open. The venom is actually squirted into the victim as the pressure of biting is applied and the teeth penetrate deep into the tissue. Although some of the large American pit-vipers have large fangs, the record seems to be held by the Gaboon Viper (*Bitis gabonica*), which possesses fangs 1 inch (2.5 centimetres) long. In the pre-First World War era, when elegant tie pins were in vogue, there developed a small demand for Gaboon Viper fangs at the London Zoo's reptile house. A number of celebrities had the 'shed' fangs mounted on a gold tie pin, probably as a good talking point!

In addition to the elapine and viperine groups, which have their fangs in the front of their mouths, there is another group of snakes known as the opisthoglyphs. These snakes have their fangs set right back in the angle of the jaw. Except for one species, the Boomslang (*Dispholidus typus*) of Africa, the back-fanged snakes are not considered very dangerous, since they frequently inflict bites without the fangs becoming effective.

All snakes regularly shed their teeth, including their fangs, but there is no safe period: reserve fangs are always waiting to take the place of those shed. Often

The Gila Monster (above left) and the Mexican Beaded Lizard (left) are the only venomous lizards.

Above With their long, narrow heads, the highly venomous mambas, such as this Jameson's Mamba (Dendroaspis jamesoni), testify to the lack of justification for the common belief that dangerous snakes have broad heads.

close examination of a snake's mouth reveals five or six reserve fangs on each side of the jaws.

Unfortunately for man, there is no hard and fast rule for recognizing venomous snakes. With lizards, it is simple. There is only one genus of venomous lizards and it contains two species which cannot possibly be mistaken for any other lizard. They are the Gila Monster (*Heloderma suspectum*), which is only found in small desert areas in Nevada, Arizona and Mexico, and the Mexican Beaded Lizard (*Heloderma horridum*) which, as its name suggests, comes from Mexico. Both are thick-set, pink and black lizards growing to about 2 feet (60 centimetres) in length. Their skin consists of round tubercles and their overall appearance is that of a mass of large pink and black beads. Their poison glands are in the lower jaw and several grooved teeth serve as their fangs. They are sluggish lizards and become very docile in captivity. Although the venom has been found to be fairly toxic, there have been no cases of human death brought about by them in America. Even the fact that they have venom appears to be a strange arrangement by nature. They feed chiefly on eggs! All the other lizards are harmless.

With the snakes one cannot always be certain whether an individual is venomous or not. Some harmless snakes closely resemble venomous ones in colour, shape and size, while others vibrate their tails among dry leaves to produce a sound similar to the rattle of deadly rattlesnakes. The cobra is readily identified when its neck is expanded to produce the hood, but confusion could arise, since there are several harmless snakes, including the Hognosed Snake (*Heterodon platyrhinos*), which flatten their necks in a threatening gesture. To some people the possession of a broad head by a snake indicates that the snake is dangerous. There is no justification for this opinion. The large vipers and pit-vipers have broad, arrow- or hatchet-shaped heads, but so do many of the non-venomous snakes, including the pythons and the Boa-Constrictor. Conversely, the mambas (*Dendroaspis* species), which must be considered to be some of the world's most venomous snakes, have very long narrow heads, eloquently described by fiction writers as coffin-shaped.

While many reptiles simply lie in wait for their food, others, which will only eat a specific creature or plant, have to hunt for it. Considering these reptiles' requirements, it is surprising that they manage to exist. A small South African snake will only eat centipedes; some of the small lizards, such as the Australian Mountain Devil (*Moloch horridus*) only eat a certain size and type of ant, while other species will only feed on tiny slugs. The two types of egg-eating snakes, *Dasypeltis* species of Africa, and Westerman's Snake (*Elachistodon westermanni*) of Bengal, are unique in the manner in which they deal with the eggs they swallow. Both types are a little thicker than an adult's finger and yet their jaws and the skin of their necks stretch sufficiently to enable eggs the size of a hen's to be swallowed. There are quite a number of snakes which supplement their usual diet of rats and mice with eggs. Several of the cobras are partial to them and the very ornate Black and Gold Tree Snake (*Boiga dendrophila*) regularly raids the nests of birds for nestlings and eggs. The eggs are swallowed whole and then digested in the stomach of these snakes. The true egg-eaters show much more expertise. They have sharp edges projecting from their vertebrae at the back of their throat and as the egg is swallowed it is pressed against them. If the egg is fresh, the contents are allowed to run down the throat; if not, they are rejected with the pelleted shell which is normally disgorged.

It is puzzling to consider how and why some of the specialist feeders ever evolved their unusual diets. We find that certain cannibal snakes will eat practically any snake or lizard that they encounter, and then another species, the Black Cribo (*Clelia clelia*) of South America, prefers eating the fierce and venomous Fer-de-lance Viper (*Bothrops atrox*) when it has a wide choice of less belligerent reptiles to feed upon. Is it possible that the Fer-de-lance has its own subtle flavour?

The King Cobras (*Naja hannah*) are not quite so particular about the species, but they will only eat snake or monitor lizard, unless a little deceit can be practised! When some years ago at London Zoo the supply of snakes, which were used as food for cannibal snakes, became depleted, we offered our 13 foot (4 metre) King Cobra some eels but it only carefully inspected them, flicking its tongue over them but making no attempt to feed. The eels were removed, placed in shed snake skins, and offered a day or two later. This time much more interest was shown and eventually the cobra struck and immediately released its jaws and did not go near the eels again. I did eventually manage to encourage it to feed on 'beef-strip snakes' which we prepared by placing 30 inch (77 centimetre) long strips of meat into shed snake skins and allowing other snakes to slither around them, imparting a snaky odour! These 'beef sausage snakes' did not replace real snakes, as beef would not have provided the cobras with a balanced diet, but they did eke out our supplies of food snakes.

There is a good deal of discrimination in the choice of food by individual reptiles. It is often observed in captivity, but it is difficult to assess under natural conditions. One finds, even among the snakes of the same litter, that the preference of one individual may be rats or mice, while others prefer feathered creatures.

The snakes are well equipped for searching out their food when needs be. In the roof of the mouth they have a device known as Jacobson's Organ which, when used in conjunction with their forked tongue, helps them smell out warm-blooded prey which may be lurking in burrows. The pit-vipers of both the Far East and the New World have other aids. Just in front of their eyes they have heat receptive pits. These are sensitive to the heat rays emanating from the body of a warm-blooded animal. A few reptiles are able to trap their food with particularly intriguing devices. The largest of the snapping turtles, the Alligator Snapper (*Macrochelys temminckii*), has a pink appendage on the centre of its tongue. Only attached by the middle, its ends wriggle about like a live worm when the snapper's mouth is open under water, enticing fishes to come within easy reach. The Tentacled Snake (*Erpeton tentaculatus*) found in Thailand also goes angling with two scaly tentacles on its nose. The Twig Snake (*Thelotornis kirtlandi*), which is so aptly named, also uses a lure to capture the small, agile lizards upon which it feeds. The tips of its flexible forked tongue are bright red or orange and they are waved about in a quivering manner, attracting the attention of inquisitive lizards, which would normally not allow the snake to come too close.

Camouflage plays a large part in helping reptiles to obtain their food, as well as being a protective device. Colour and shape, assisted by the animal's behaviour, enable many reptiles to blend with their surroundings and so evade detection by predator or prey. Certain reptiles have developed a striking resemblance to leaves, twigs, bark, sand and rocks, for example.

Many small lizards, in particular, are well camouflaged. The geckos, the only family of lizards which produce vocal sounds, provide an excellent example. They are a very large group of lizards and are represented in all the warmer parts of the world. Most of the family are fairly small. In fact, the smallest lizard in the world, *Sphaerodactylus parthenopium* of the West Indies, which is less than 1 inch (2.5 centimetres) long, is a gecko. They are efficient at changing colour; it is a common occurrence to see a grey individual run up a grey wall and then scamper across the white ceiling as a white specimen. The palm gecko (*Phelsuma* species) is the most beautiful of these lizards and is found in Madagascar. It is a soft, velvety, emerald green with bright red spots and yet it becomes hardly noticeable as it crawls amongst the dark green foliage. The strangest of the geckos is the Parachute, or Flying Gecko (*Ptychozoon kuhli*), which has a fringe of skin stretched around its body and limbs. When it lies on a branch, the fringe 'welds' into the bark so well that it

Scarcely visible, a Flying Gecko remains motionless on the trunk of a tree. The patterning of the skin and the flattening of the body against the bark render this reptile almost perfectly camouflaged.

Overleaf When disturbed the Frilled Lizard erects a ruff of brilliantly coloured skin around its neck and opens its yellow mouth.

is difficult to see the lizard even if one knows where to look. It cannot fly, but with skin outstretched, it is able to glide to the ground from high trees, a feat which it shares with other small lizards also found in South East Asia, the flying dragons of the genus *Draco*. They are dull brown or greyish lizards, similar to the Parachute Gecko until they 'take off'. Then their brightly coloured 'wings' which are stretched each side of their bodies unfold.

Mimicry is an important means of protection whereby a harmless creature can derive benefit from resembling a dangerous one. Certain reptiles employ this means of protection.

The coloration of the venomous coral snake of the southern United States (*Micrurus fulvius*) is copied, though not exactly, by several harmless snakes. Both forms, venomous and harmless, have alternating bands of red, black and yellow along the length of the body. However, in the venomous form the yellow and red bands are adjacent, while in the harmless form black separates these two colours. Despite this inaccuracy in the copying, the harmless snakes presumably derive some protection from it.

More accurate mimicry is shown by the harmless *Simophis rhinostoma*, which mimics another poisonous coral snake, *Micrurus frontalis*. Both these Brazilian snakes have alternating bands of red, black and yellow again. In this case the sequence is identical in the two snakes.

A similar form of protection might be afforded the harmless king snakes (*Lampropeltis* species) and rat snakes (*Elaphe* species), under certain conditions. As already mentioned, these snakes, when disturbed, vibrate their tails and if this occurs amongst dry leaves the sound produced is not unlike that resulting from the rattle of dry segments in the tail of the venomous rattlesnakes.

Many reptiles are capable of putting on displays of aggression to intimidate a would-be predator, or an intruder into their territory. Often this aggressive behaviour is purely bluff, since the animal is quite harmless. Colour and colour pattern play an important part in these aggressive displays.

An Australian agamid lizard, the Frilled Lizard (*Chlamydosaurus kingi*) is grey-brown and grows up to 3 feet (1 metre) in length. One of its favourite resting places is an old tree stump, where it becomes almost imperceptible, until disturbed. Then it suddenly erects a ruff of brilliantly coloured skin around its neck. The gaping yellow mouth and expanded frill present an awe-inspiring sight.

A close relative of this lizard is the Bearded Lizard

The Bearded Lizard of South Australia gets its name from the bristly growth of skin under its chin. This 'beard' can be erected, presumably to intimidate the lizard's adversaries.

(*Amphibolurus barbatus*) of South Australia. It is not as large as its relative and instead of having a ruff completely encircling its neck it has a bristly one under its chin, from which it gets its name. Presumably this erected beard is designed to intimidate the creature's enemies. It most probably does, but I think that it creates a rather benevolent expression, which is perhaps in keeping with the lizard's nature, for it rarely attempts to bite even when picked up.

Some African races treat the chameleons with awe. This is understandable to a certain extent, if one watches these strange creatures in their natural surroundings. They never rush about like many of the lizards. Often, they just remain in one position, looking rather like a leaf. If any movement occurs near them, only their turretted eyes move round into focus. When they walk along a branch they sway in a peculiar manner, with two steps forward and then a slight hesitation. The weirdness is accentuated in the species which have horns above their eyes, or on the ends of their nose. Especially weird are the great Madagascan specimens which have huge sail fins along their backs and casques on top of their heads, reminding one of the early horned dinosaurs. All the chameleons live a solitary life, preferring to occupy their own particular tree or shrub. The males become quite ferocious when another male trespasses upon their territory, and put on a good display of aggression. They enhance their normal rather grotesque appearance by inflating the body, raising the small flaps near the ears, and opening the mouth in a threatening manner. If this is not sufficient to divert the intruder, a firmer approach is taken, with pushing and jousting in the horned species.

All these lizards are relatively harmless, their displays of aggression being mainly bluff. Certain harmless and, rather surprisingly, certain venomous snakes also resort to this form of bluff. Rather than fighting, the venomous forms perform aggressive-looking movements which are, in fact, quite harmless. However, since they are well able to defend themselves by striking with their fangs, this behaviour should perhaps be described as warning behaviour. We have already discussed the ability of the cobras and certain harmless snakes to flatten the neck in a threatening gesture. Since the cobras are venomous snakes, their behaviour can be regarded as warning behaviour, while that of the harmless forms can be regarded as bluff. An obvious example of warning behaviour is the vibrating of the tail by rattlesnakes.

Inflation of the body is quite commonly employed in the aggressive displays of snakes, to make the animal appear larger and more menacing. The Puff Adder (*Bitis arietans*) provides a good example of this type of behaviour. Some snakes suddenly display bright colours when confronted by an adversary. The Red-tailed Pipe Snake (*Cylindrophis rufus*) of South East Asia raises its bright red tail and waves it aloft. Hissing

A Cape Cobra with the front part of the body raised off the ground and the hood erect. This raising of the body and flattening of the neck to produce the hood is an example of aggressive display. Since this snake is highly venomous, the action may be regarded as a warning gesture, as distinct from the display of bluff which is enacted by various harmless reptiles.

frequently accompanies these displays. The Bull Snake (*Pituophis catenifer*) makes a particularly loud noise by blowing air against a flap of flesh, just in front of the opening to the windpipe.

Aggressive displays are frequently associated with courtship. At such times a male reptile is particularly sensitive to intrusion by other males into its territory. Defence of territory is particularly well shown by the lizards. The bright colours that enhance the aggressive displays also serve to attract the females. This is again especially true of the lizards.

Courtship and breeding habits take various forms among the reptiles. The large male crocodilians become extremely vociferous at breeding times, and at night they bellow like bulls. Often several individuals take up these challenges and the sound carries an incredible distance. At the same time a strong odour of musk permeates the air from their throat glands, attracting interested females which eventually glide along to accept advances from the males. These generally consist of snout rubbing snout and the occasional bite on the neck or across the broad base of the tail. This looks as if it should be quite damaging, but actually the procedure is fairly gentle, unless intruding males appear on the scene, when even death can result.

The pairing takes place in the water and becomes quite an acrobatic feat.

The crocodile deposits its eggs in a sand bank above water level. They are placed in a scooped out hollow and then covered over. The forty or more eggs are watched over by the female for the whole three months of the incubation, and at this time she is inclined to be very aggressive. The alligator is more ambitious with nest building. A site is chosen near the river bank and plant debris is collected together to form a large mound, sometimes as much as 3 feet (1 metre) high. The eggs are laid and more vegetation is scraped over them. The female sometimes constructs a tunnel, close to the nest, where she takes up guard duties. There is some doubt as to whether she actually assists the young to reach the surface of the nest, which may mean a crawl of 8 inches (20 centimetres), but once they emerge and commence 'croaking' she keeps a careful watch over them for several months, driving away other alligators intent on committing infanticide. There is little maternal instinct shown by other reptiles.

Most snake species lead a solitary life and it is surprising that they are able to find partners when required. The crocodilians and the geckos can at least make themselves heard, but the male snakes have to rely largely upon finding traces of 'scent' left behind by the female. In some species of snake, notably the cobras, a form of pre-nuptial dancing takes place between the sexes. The dancers, after simple preliminaries, rear their heads together high above the ground with a twisting and swaying movement. The same type of ritual is performed by the Aesculapian Snake (*Elaphe longissima*), which is found in Europe. At first the females of this species use 'hard to get' tactics by dodging about, then male and female rear up facing each other and a kind of mock fight is enacted for hours before mating takes place. This form of behaviour, when two snakes rear up facing each other, is often observed among the rattlesnakes and the smaller vipers, but on close observation both the dancers are found to be male. It is thought that these 'combat dances' of male snakes are the result of rivalry over a mate or territory. The commonest courtship behaviour is less spectacular. It consists of the male weaving his body alongside the female, flicking his tongue and pressing his chin along her back until he reaches her head. If the female does not slither away in a hurry, he commences a nudging action and then coils around her until tails entwine and pairing takes place. The pythons and Boa Constrictors have one small advantage over other snakes. At the end of the body, where it joins the tail, the male has two small claws (they are vestigial limbs) which during courtship are used for playfully scratching the back of the female.

Most species of snakes are egg-layers, usually laying the soft parchment-like eggs several months after mating. The exact time interval varies a great deal. In

A female European Adder with her day-old young. The eggs of this species are retained, and therefore protected, within the body of the female until the young are at the point of hatching.

some species the eggs may be retained for a long time so that when laid they are fairly advanced and thus the incubation period is shortened. In other species a full three months may be required between laying and hatching. Very few snakes make any attempt at constructing a nest for their eggs: generally they scrape a hole in the ground or in a dead tree stump. One snake which does build a nest is the King Cobra. The female collects together a mass of brushwood and leaves in which she then deposits her eggs. It is reported that she remains on top of the nest during the whole incubation period. The pythons remain tightly coiled around their clutch of eggs, which may number sixty or more, for about sixty days, only leaving them for very short periods. It has been discovered that their body temperature increases a few degrees during this time, which is strange for a cold-blooded animal that normally relies on its surroundings to control its temperature. Quite a number of snakes enlist the aid of the heat generated by rotting vegetable matter to incubate their eggs. In districts where common Grass Snakes (*Natrix natrix*)

flourish, often clutches of thirty or forty eggs can be found buried in the farm yard dung heaps during July. As with all the reptiles, very few of the litter will reach maturity. Even roosters will eat the young Grass Snakes as they hatch. In company with many other reptiles, the snakes are equipped with a small egg tooth on the end of their nose, which is used to cut their way out of the egg. It projects like a tiny knife blade and is only capable of making one or two slits. It then falls off. I have been able to observe several clutches of python eggs hatching, and have found that the snakes did not immediately leave the shell after having slit it open. Sometimes they would remain inside with head extended for a couple of days, pulling right back inside the shell if disturbed. On a few occasions, I have seen the youngsters which had already emerged slither back inside the egg case again, with some difficulty, and remain there for several hours.

Some species of snake give birth to live young, that is, the eggs are retained, and therefore protected, in the female's body until the point of hatching. The European Adder (*Vipera berus*) produces its young in this way, as do the boas.

All snakes, whether born alive or from eggs, are able to fend for themselves from the very beginning. The constrictors are able to constrict and the venomous

snakes are able to inflict a poisonous bite. Young vipers and pit-vipers, for instance, not only have well developed poison fangs at birth, but also a supply of venom for immediate use. No female snake feeds its young or shows very much maternal instinct. However, the litter may stay with her for a few days as I found when a litter of forty-two Western Boas (*Constrictor occidentalis*) were born at the London Zoo. In this case the female remained in the vicinity of the young during the first few hours of their being born and behaved aggressively towards anyone approaching them. Even when removed from them, she quickly returned, but this interest in her offspring was not of a lasting nature.

Colour differences frequently exist between male and female lizards. They may be permanent, seasonal or momentary. Usually it is the males that are brightly coloured. They are prone to giving sexual displays of stereotyped movements which enhance the effect of their bright coloration. These displays serve to intimidate other males as well as to attract females.

Both egg-laying and live-bearing habits are found among the lizard group. In either event, fewer offspring are produced than in other reptile groups. If eggs are laid the nest is generally very simple, the main requirement being comparative uniformity of temperature and humidity. The egg-laying habits of geckos are rather interesting. The eggs are laid aloft, in cracks of bark or walls, for example. When laid they are coated in a substance which becomes sticky on drying, enabling the female to attach them firmly to the surface on which they are laid. Some lizards lay their eggs in termite nests, while the females of egg-laying species of chameleon bury their eggs. About eight weeks after pairing, the female tunnels a hole, sometimes 1 foot (30 centimetres) long, under a bush. She then lays fifteen or more eggs and replaces the soil as she returns to the entrance. The eggs may take from six to eleven months to hatch. There is little parental care of the young among lizards, but some skinks of the genus *Eumeces*, notably the Five-lined Skink (*E. fasciatus*) and the Great Plains Skink (*E. obsoletus*), not only guard and turn their eggs during incubation, but also clean the young with their tongue and protect them while they feed.

Most skinks give birth to live young which are able to fend for themselves within a few hours of birth. I have witnessed the fascinating sight of a dozen young Sand Fish (*Scincus scincus*) travelling just below the surface of a sandy waste, in search of tiny insects. Some chameleons also give birth to live young, which emerge

A female Elliot's Dwarf Chameleon (Chameleo bitaeniatus elloti) with some of her young, which are less than a day old. It is fascinating to watch such minute, perfect replicas of the adults climbing thin twigs and shooting out their tongues to catch small insects.

Below A herbivorous Greek Tortoise takes a meal of lettuce.

Below right A chameleon devours a cricket, after catching it on the sticky end of its long, muscular tongue.

from tiny transparent 'envelopes'. Again it is a fascinating sight to see these minute creatures, perfect replicas of their parents, climbing thin twigs within minutes of being born, and later shooting out their tongues to catch mosquitoes.

The chelonians are the most gregarious of the reptiles. A large old Snapping Turtle (*Chelydra serpentina*) or Leatherback (*Dermochelys coriacea*) may live a solitary existence, lying in the mud at the bottom of a pool, but generally the tortoises, turtles and terrapins live a more sociable life than the snakes.

Prior to mating, the male land tortoise indulges in a little horse-play. He knocks the female's shell with his own shell to gain her attention. When she eventually stretches out her head and neck to see the cause of the banging, she may receive a couple of bites on her neck or legs.

There is a little more finesse in the courtship of some of the terrapins. Male painted terrapins (genus *Chrysemys*) and male sliders (genus *Pseudemys*), of America, grow extra long toe nails in the breeding season and perform a 'fan dance'. As the male swims in front of the female, he waves his feet and claws in a rhythmic motion, caressing her head and neck with his long claws. If the performance has sufficient charm, they both swim away to a quieter corner of the pool to mate, and fertile eggs will be laid some months later. It is an interesting fact that with the chelonians, as with certain other reptiles, one pairing is sufficient to fertilize eggs for several seasons. It has happened that female tortoises which have lived alone for two years or more have produced fertile eggs that have subsequently hatched.

Certain reptiles have evolved unique and fascinating adaptations to a particular way of life.

All the geckos have feet well adapted to the type of terrain in which they live. Some of the desert species have fringes of skin on their feet, enabling them to travel over sand more easily. A number of species, which climb walls and rocks and so forth, have small pads of laminated skin on the base of their feet. The increased friction allows them to take a firm grip on any smooth surface, even glass.

We have already discussed the Flying Gecko and the flying dragons, with their fold of skin along the side of the body which, when stretched, permits them to glide to the ground from high trees.

The skinks comprise one of the largest families of lizard. They are numerous throughout the warm countries of the world. Most of their life is spent underground and they are able to dig efficiently with their shovel-like feet and noses. One beautiful golden species, *Scincus scincus*, is so well adapted to a subterranean life that it can travel faster through the sand than on top of it. In Egypt it has come to be known as the Sand Fish.

There are about sixty species of chameleon in the

Above left Male painted terrapins and sliders, such as this Red-eared Terrapin, grow long toe-nails in the breeding season, with which to caress the female's head and neck.

Left Skinks spend most of their life underground and are able to dig efficiently with the feet and nose.

Top The pads of laminated skin on the base of the feet of the Flying Gecko enable it to grip any surface.

Above The feet of the chameleon are bifurcated to enable it to take a firm grip when climbing.

Left An American Alligator eats a Garfish.

Many reptiles, such as the Iguana (below left) and Jackson's Chameleon (below), are capable of putting on displays of aggression to intimidate a would-be predator or an intruder into their territory.

world. One is found in southern Europe; but the majority are found in Africa and Madagascar. A few species are about 1 inch (2.5 centimetres) in length and live on the ground, but in general they are larger and live in trees and bushes. There are some fantastic specimens in Madagascar reaching 2 feet (60 centimetres) in length and capable of eating mice and small birds. There are several features which are unique to the chameleons. No other lizards have quite the same type of tongue, feet or eyes. The tongue is approximately the same length as the lizard's body and has a club-shaped end which is both sticky and muscular. It is capable of being rapidly projected towards an insect, which is caught and brought back to the mouth. The feet of the chameleon are bifurcated, with the toes forming two opposing groups of two and three, rather similar to those of the parrot. This adaptation enables the chameleon to take a firm grip when climbing on branches and twigs. The eyes are turretted and capable of being swivelled around independently of one another. These slow-moving lizards are thus well adapted to catching the most elusive insects.

One of the more interesting adaptations of the crocodilians is the positioning of the nostrils on top of the head. This enables the animal to remain completely submerged except for the nostrils, which just protrude from the water so that it can breathe. A similar adaptation is seen in the hippopotamus.

We have already discussed the many adaptations of snakes for locating, overpowering and eating their prey. Jacobson's organ is very highly developed in snakes, and in conjunction with the long bifid tongue it forms an efficient scent-detecting organ. The heat-detecting organ of the pit-vipers is a unique adaptation for locating warm-blooded prey. The venomous bite and the constricting ability of snakes can be regarded as compensation for the lack of limbs and powerful teeth. Again this lack of limbs and tearing teeth can be said to have resulted in the snake's strange method of eating, the dislocation of the jaws and the formation of the bend behind the head.

The protective shell is the chelonian's most obvious adaptation. This heavy armour, the rather pillar-like legs and the animal's slow-moving habits are all closely interrelated.

Unique physical characteristics and strange behaviour patterns make the reptile group a fascinating one to study.

The protective shell is the chelonian's most obvious adaptation to its particular way of life. The upper shell or carapace is joined by a bridge at each side to the lower shell or plastron. The Indian Starred Tortoise has a highly domed carapace and on each creamy coloured shield radiating lines form the star pattern which has given the animal its common name.

*Above left A warning of the deadly bite of the Canebrake
Rattlesnake (Crotalus horridus atricaudatus), and other
rattlesnakes, is given by the vibrating of the tip of the tail,
the rattle.*

*Left Smooth Green Snakes (Opheodrys vernalis vernalis)
hatching.*

Above A green Turtle struggles out of its egg shell.

Reptiles as Pets

After consideration and despite misgivings, I have given this chapter the title of 'Reptiles as Pets'. I do not like it, however. I have always considered that the word 'pet' should only be used to denote a friendly, furred or feathered animal which has sufficient intelligence to recognize its owner and is endowed with very few troublesome vices. The word 'pet' has now become a most hackneyed term, used to describe practically any animal, friendly or otherwise, which is kept in domestic surroundings.

There is one aspect of pet-keeping which should not exist, whether the creatures involved are warm- or cold-blooded, and that is cruelty. It is more obvious when it affects cats and dogs and other warm-blooded animals but a tremendous amount of cruelty is meted out to the lower orders of animals. It is not always intentional and, in fact, thoughtlessness and lack of knowledge play the greatest parts.

There is little excuse for a lack of knowledge leading to cruelty, since information and helpful advice can be readily and freely obtained from many sources. Animal protection and zoological societies often assist with the welfare of animals by providing leaflets and practical help. Libraries can supply suitable literature and they often arrange lectures by qualified personnel.

There is one point that must be stressed about the keeping of pets, especially reptiles. The animal's needs, including those of accommodation, food and temperature, and whether or not it will be readily accepted into the household must be considered *before* it is obtained. This may seem obvious, but so often animals are bought, because they look cute, by people who have no idea of their requirements. Any animal obtained for this reason alone is certainly going to be less popular should its appearance change for the worse, and then it becomes an embarrassment to its owner. It is not always possible for the local zoo or animal welfare society to find other accommodation and eventually the poor creature is destroyed.

The crocodilians have had, and still are having, rather a bad deal as pets. In the southern United States baby Mississippi Alligators (*Alligator mississippiensis*) or their eggs were collected and reared. Their owners gained a lot of satisfaction and knowledge in the process. Young alligators, about 8 inches (20 centimetres) long at birth, have a bright, perky, almost bird-like appearance. They soon become used to being handled and do not bite. It was not very long before commercially-minded people realized the potential of the young crocodilians and, after suitable advertising campaigns, they were sold in chain-stores and by mail-order firms as novelties. The luckier ones were well cared for and thrived, but the majority died after the first few months, when the novelty had worn off and they had begun to be neglected. Those which lived caused problems for their owners. As they grew, more

living space was required, and if room was limited the pet alligator had to be disposed of. Some were dumped in rivers and ponds in cool areas and consequently died. It was the New York sewer-men who highlighted the fact that many problem alligators were being put down drains and manholes, eventually finding their way into the labyrinths of the sewers. There was no danger to the sewer-men, as the strong caustics soon destroyed the creatures, but it did help to bring legislation protecting the young alligators from exploitation. The Caiman Alligator (*Caiman scelrops*) of South America is now being treated in the same way, not only in America but also in Britain, where hundreds are imported and sold in pet stores for a pound or two each.

Caiman Alligators live in the tropical waters of Colombia and Guyana and are comparatively hardy if kept warm. When about 6 or 7 inches (15 centimetres) in length they can easily be housed and are often sold in a plastic container, entirely unsuitable for the purpose. These quaint little creatures are not as docile as the Mississippi Alligator and are inclined to become more belligerent as they grow larger. Having already increased the size of their tanks several times, some owners then decide to part with their pet, only to find that it has become a 'white elephant'. The Zoological Society of London receives hundreds of requests every year for accommodation for unwanted pet caimans, but space at the zoo is limited and they are, reluctantly, refused. One wonders how many of these creatures go down the London sewers. A few are cast into ponds and rivers and one or two have been seen floating dead in the Thames. British waters are much too cold for them to live in and so their lives are cut short well before they reach their full size of about 6 feet (2 metres).

Pet chelonians (tortoises, terrapins and turtles) are treated a little better than the crocodilians, although there is still much suffering inflicted upon them. The Greek Tortoises (*Testudo graeca*) and their close relatives the Herman Tortoises (*Testudo hermanni*) are exported in their millions from the Mediterranean region of North Africa and Balkan countries to countries all over Europe, and this trade has caused extinction in some areas. Chelonians are sun-loving and need warmth, but many are sold in countries which have only a short summer. A few summer months are often not long enough to enable them to feed sufficiently well for successful hibernation, and they die at the end of one season, instead of living the fifty years or more which is their allotted span. If these

Previous page A little boy with the family pet, an African Python (Python sebae).

While young Mississippi Alligators make delightful pets, large adults provide their owners with many problems.

are well cared for they have a certain charm and often appear to recognize their guardians.

One or two salient points regarding the keeping of Greek Tortoises should be made. A warm, sunny garden is absolutely necessary; a close-boarded fence or close-wired netting boundary is needed to prevent wandering; and a cool, dry, vermin-proof shed or outhouse should be provided, so that the tortoises can hibernate until late spring, safe from frost. A vermin-proof shed is particularly important, since I have known hibernating tortoises to be eaten alive by rats during a hard winter. Successful hibernation can only be attained if the tortoise commences its sleep in a fit condition. If insufficient food has been taken prior to hibernation, it will not live, and it is necessary to encourage feeding by offering little extras, such as soft fruits and bread and milk, in addition to the normal vegetable diet.

These Mediterranean tortoises will breed in captivity during very warm summers in Britain and their courtship is fascinating. One of the best descriptions I have read is in Gerald Durrell's book 'My Family and other Animals'. I will not attempt to describe the action but I do suggest that, if you decide to keep a tortoise, you should purchase a male and female. It is so much more interesting to watch a pair, even if they never produce an egg. On hot days they show an almost unbelievable amount of activity, rushing after each other and banging their shells together and often making little croaking noises when they meet. But these pleasures are only for the fortunate tortoises which are given the run of a garden. The greatest number end up in little sunless back yards without any vegetation and where they are expected to fend for themselves. I have even heard vendors of these unfortunate reptiles describe their beetle-catching qualities and suggest that they should be placed in a cellar as destroyers of cockroaches!

Although a sunny, walled garden is ideal, a large wired or boarded enclosure, placed in the sunniest spot of the garden and containing a small shelter will suffice. On no account should tortoises be tethered. The practice of drilling a hole on the edge of the shell and attaching a string is not at all wise, since the line becomes entangled with their legs. Feeding should present no problems. They will eat lettuce, dandelions, various grasses and low-growing plants and can be given a variety of soft fruits and vegetables. They are inclined to be scavengers under normal conditions and so occasionally they can be given a little bread and milk, a little minced meat and even small pieces of cheese to make up for any deficiency in their diet when scavenging is not possible. If a tortoise has fed well, by the end of the summer one should be able to observe a plumpness around the shoulders and legs, denoting the fat reserves necessary for successful hibernation. In northern temperate climates tortoises tend to become

Left Young Mississippi Alligators are engaging little creatures.

Above The docile tortoise is perhaps the most popular of all reptilian pets.

lethargic after the end of September or October and when this happens they will no longer feed. They should then be installed in a ventilated box, packed with hay, straw or leaves and placed in a cool shed. Do not unnecessarily disturb them but make sure that heavy frosts do not affect them. During a very mild winter if the temperature increases they may get a little restless but they will not feed and should be left to become dormant again.

In the spring, when the weather has become warm and settled, tortoises will once more become active. At this time they should receive several warm baths, which are shallow enough to enable them to extend their heads above the water-line. A little attention is often needed around the mouth and eyes. Mucus tends to gum up the lids and jaws which should be carefully bathed until free. Sometimes it is necessary to lightly press a sharpened matchstick around the jaws before they can be opened, but great care must be exercised, pressing from below the chin upwards as the top jaw overlaps the lower jaw, but this should not be done until the warm water has softened the mucus.

Newly imported tortoises often lay eggs and these can be hatched out. They need to be placed in sand, with about 1 inch (2.5 centimetres) of covering, and kept at a temperature of 26°C without being turned for approximately eight weeks. The infant tortoises are soft-shelled replicas of the adults and need to be kept in a well illuminated receptacle at a temperature of 24°C to 26°C for the first year or two of their life. Their food should be finely chopped lettuce, cabbage and soft fruits, and these can be liberally sprinkled with glucose. Cytocon or other vitamin B.12 products are beneficial to them and will often help to restore a lost

Left The Greek Tortoise needs a warm sunny garden.

Above The Herman Tortoise is closely related to the Greek Tortoise.

appetite, a very common happening with these small reptiles.

There are a few other species of land tortoises offered for sale as pets in addition to those we have grouped as Mediterranean ones. The Starred Tortoise (*Testudo elegans*) is sometimes to be found in pet stores. It is one of the most attractive of the hard-shelled chelonians, having a highly domed carapace with radiating lines forming the star pattern, from which it gets its name, on each creamy coloured shield. They come from India and Ceylon and cannot survive outdoors in northern temperate climates, except perhaps for the short periods of a very hot summer. If a large vivarium can be obtained with some form of heating (suspended electric bulbs, especially infra-red, are suitable), the Starred Tortoise makes an interesting pet. Sometimes these tortoises have blemished shells;

they have cracked and healed again. It is generally accepted that these injuries were caused by Indian birds of prey. These are partial to tortoise flesh and obtain it by taking the tortoise aloft and dropping it. The cracked-shelled ones are those which escaped! It is an explanation which is certainly true in many cases, but some shells have more likely been damaged in automobile accidents.

Another land tortoise which has appeared for sale in large numbers in the last four or five years is the Horsfield Tortoise (*Testudo horsfieldi*), which is found in Afghanistan and the Kirghiz Steppes. It is somewhat similar to the Mediterranean tortoises, but can be easily distinguished from other species by the fact that it has four claws on its feet instead of five. Outside their own habitat, they were previously only seen in zoo reptile houses and were often considered semi-rare, but now they are exported from Russia in great numbers. Although they are more active at lower temperatures than the other species mentioned, they must have very dry conditions and for this reason they are not likely to survive in Britain or other countries

67

with a comparable climate. They have one character-istic in which they surpass other land tortoises, and that is their ability to climb. If it is possible for them to get a grip with their front feet, it is remarkable how they will scale fairly high, vertical, wire-netting fences. They are most persistent in their endeavours. I have watched them climb, fall back and climb again until they have succeeded. Other tortoises would have been deterred by the fence and would not even have at-tempted to climb. The Horsfield Tortoise can be kept successfully for many years in a dry glass-house with a floor of dry sand, on which a few rocks are dotted, and an old tree stump for shelter. An infra-red lamp, pro-viding a warm area in which it can lie, is essential. This is an ideal way of keeping the land tortoises, and if a sunken pool is built in a glass-house, many other small reptiles may be housed in addition.

The Carolina Box Tortoise (*Terrapene carolina*) is an alert little tortoise to keep. In parts of the United States they are exceedingly numerous and are often kept as pets. They need marshy conditions and are fairly easy to feed if the owner lives out of town. Although they are reputed to prefer fungi to other foods, I have found that they choose earthworms in preference to practically anything else, and I have had

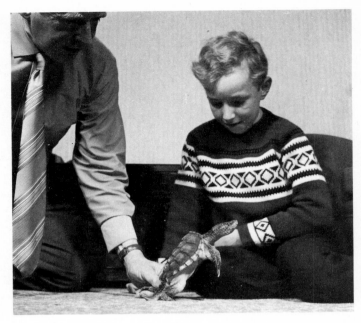

Above The author shows a young friend his Snapping Turtle.

Below Pet shops sometimes sell Starred Tortoises.

Below right The Tortoise will eat a variety of soft fruits and vegetables as well as grass and dandelions.

individuals which lived for twelve years or more on nothing but earthworms. They have received the name of Box Tortoise because of the hinges on the lower shell which enable them to close up both ends and so protect head and limbs. Their shells (carapaces) are usually a chestnut brown with golden yellow radiating lines or spots. They very rarely exceed 6 inches (15 centimetres) in length. In some areas of the United States they were eaten. It is reported that, some years ago, hungry miners at Scranton fed on Box Tortoise meat and became seriously ill afterwards. It appears that the tortoises had previously fed on poisonous toadstools without any ill effects to themselves!

When they have been in captivity a short time these tortoises become friendly towards their keepers and stretch their heads out instead of 'boxing up'. However, if several tortoises are kept together they often show a belligerent attitude to each other at feeding times and I have seen them bite each other with their sharp-hooked beaks. On one occasion an unfortunate individual lost a small piece of its neck!

Overleaf The Carolina Box Tortoise is often kept as a pet in the United States.

The European Pond Tortoise (*Emys orbicularis*) and the Spanish Terrapin (*Clemmys leprosa*) are regularly imported into Britain in the spring. Whereas a few years ago adult specimens arrived from Italy, Spain and North Africa, now half grown specimens or hatchlings are arriving, which suggests that the collectors are 'scraping the bottom of the barrel'. A few years ago the Pond Tortoise was very common throughout southern and middle Europe, but now it has completely disappeared from districts where it was once exceedingly numerous, and it is difficult to pinpoint the reason. It is understandable that they have disappeared from areas where they were collected for the pet trade so intensively that even small children helped in the searches, but they have also disappeared from parks where this type of exploitation has not taken place.

In captivity these terrapins are fairly hardy if given the right attention. The very small ones should be housed in an aquarium or even a plastic washing-up bowl. Deep water is not necessary or desirable, but if possible rainwater or tap water which has been left to stand for a few days should be used. Standing assists the removal of the chlorine which has been added to tap water and which is harmful to the terrapin's eyes.

Large Pond Tortoises can be successfully kept in a garden pond during the summer and can remain there if the water is sufficiently deep, 2 to 3 feet (60 to 90 centimetres) at least, and if the bottom is muddy. During the winter they will hibernate in the mud or they can be placed in a box and treated in the same way as the land tortoises. If terrapins are kept in an aquarium in the house they must be near a window and have an electric bulb suspended above them for extra illumination, especially during dull days. The water temperature should fluctuate between 20°C and 26°C. The water needs to be just deep enough to allow the terrapins to swim freely and pieces of rock should be arranged in it to enable them to sit above water level. A feed three times each week is ample. No more than the animals can eat should be given, otherwise the water becomes unnecessarily fouled up. Tinned dog and cat food can figure largely on their menu with the addition of brown bread, cheese, raw liver and raw fish. They love the inside of the latter, but it makes a mess in the aquarium. The special dried turtle food should not be purchased. It is not readily eaten and mainly contains unsuitable foods. Nearly all the small terrapins I have seen suffering from malnutrition have had this dried food offered to them and little else.

The terrapins which are mostly sold today are the baby Red-eared Terrapins (*Pseudemys scripta elegans*) and some close relatives, such as Troost's Terrapin (*Pseudemys scripta*). To a lesser extent the Southern Painted Terrapin (*Chrysemys picta doisalis*) is also marketed as a pet. Besides being kept as pets in their native North America, these terrapins are also exported to Europe. Several hundred individuals, a little over 1 inch (2.5 centimetres) across and often only a few weeks old, are wrapped in damp moss and transported in plastic containers. At this size terrapins are the most charming of all the small aquatic animals. The baby Red-eared Terrapins have a bright red flash just behind the eye, with a pale green ridged shell. The plastron or under shell is ivory in colour and has irregular eye-like spots. The Painted Terrapins have smooth semi-polished shells, with generally a dark reddish patterning on the carapace, a red stripe running across the back, and yellow flashes on the side of the head. It is their attractive size and colouring that is really their undoing, since they are frequently purchased because they look rather bizarre and novel. The fact that they are alive and need care and attention is often overlooked. Most of these little creatures die in their first year. They are really not very difficult to rear; they usually die so soon because the owners were given the wrong information or it was too much trouble to find out what these terrapins required in the

The most commonly kept terrapin is the Red-eared Terrapin, so named because the juveniles have a bright red flash just behind the eye. This fades with age.

Below Red-eared Terrapins can live in a garden pool during the summer months.

Right It is fascinating to watch a chameleon shoot out its long tongue to capture an insect some distance away. The trouble involved in feeding these reptiles is well worthwhile.

way of food and housing. If imported into northern temperate climates like that of Britain, it is imperative that the young ones are kept in warm water at about 25°C. If they are too cold they become torpid and will not feed. Their aquarium or bowl should be placed in a sunny position and have extra lighting above on dull days. Their normal food is small water creatures, worms, insects and small fishes, but they will thrive on the food suggested for the European terrapins.

These American terrapins will eventually grow to adults of 6 to 8 inches (15 to 20 centimetres) long but it will take five years or even longer and then they will need a very large aquarium in which to swim. During the summer they can live in a garden pool, but it should be remembered that they will eat any small fishes they might find in it.

In the winter they will hibernate if the pool is deep and has mud on the bottom, but it is preferable to allow them to hibernate similarly to the land tortoises, using damp leaves instead of hay and straw. If there are the facilities to maintain summer temperatures in winter, they will forgo their hibernation.

As the Red-eared Terrapins grow older, the red flashes on the head fade so that they become less attractive to look at. It is at this time that many owners become tired of them and have great difficulty in finding someone willing to give them a home.

Often young terrapins are sold as miniatures, and I recently saw a number which were purchased in Hong Kong as Miniature Chinese Turtles. They had been covered in paint and varnish, which would have proved fatal if it had not been carefully scraped off.

Some would-be reptile keepers disdain tortoises and terrapins and would prefer to keep lizards or snakes.

The Slow-worm makes an ideal reptilian pet. They are seldom offered for sale, but can sometimes be collected on disused railway embankments.

The Slow-worm or Blindworm (*Anguis fragilis*) makes an ideal reptile pet. It is a legless lizard, although it could be mistaken for a small snake. They are usually about 12 inches (30 centimetres) in length, and have a shiny, bronze appearance. Some specimens have blue markings down the back and look most attractive. They are not often offered for sale, but they can sometimes be collected on disused railway embankments, where they lie in the sun on tufts of grass. They were relatively numerous at one time but intensive weed-killing by the railway authorities has taken its toll. The origin of their common name is rather obscure; they are not slow or blind, neither are they worms. They are often mistaken for small snakes. Some years ago one of the large foreign embassies in Britain sent me a pair of large chopped-up Slow-worms from an out-of-town residence that they had purchased. I was requested to identify the snakes and inform the embassy how dangerous they were!

Slow-worms are easily kept in a vivarium. Their favourite food is the tiny white slug but they will eat small earthworms and many other invertebrates. They soon settle down in a vivarium furnished with a floor of leaf mould, bark or moss, and a small dish of water. When first born, the twelve or more offspring seem to be of burnished copper but after the first season they become darker. The Slow-worms are very long-lived and an age of fifty years has more than once been recorded.

Most of the European lizards will become satisfactory inmates of the vivarium if given a reasonable amount of attention and I have often found that the commonest are the most hardy and attractive. The small Viviparous Lizard (*Lacerta vivipara*) will survive quite amicably with the Slow-worm and the European Sand Lizard (*Lacerta agilis*). The former is still numerous on the heathlands of Europe, and can often be seen on commons around London, whereas the Sand Lizard is rare in Britain. The Viviparous Lizard will breed in captivity, giving birth to up to a dozen young but the infants are difficult to rear. The most satisfactory method of dealing with the family is probably to

The Viviparous Lizard is an interesting reptile to keep as a pet, since it will readily breed in captivity. The female gives birth to up to a dozen young.

Above left The Green Lizard is a difficult reptile to keep in a vivarium but will thrive if allowed to live in near-natural conditions.

Above In captivity, the European Whip Snake (*Coluber viridi flavus*), like any of the small constricting snakes, will eat dead rats or mice.

attempt to rear one or two individuals only and to release the others in suitable terrain to fend for themselves. At least it gives them a chance of survival and it is very rewarding in a few seasons to find that one has started a new colony.

The Wall Lizard (*Lacerta muralis*) is found throughout the warmer parts of Europe. There are numerous sub-species and races and although they do not differ greatly in size, being from 6 to 8 inches (15 to 20 centimetres) in length, their colouring and patterning are fascinating, ranging from palest green chequering to black with brilliant blue or orange undersides. Lizards with the latter colouring are found on the rocky islands in the Mediterranean. Wall Lizards are very agile creatures and great care is needed in servicing their vivarium to prevent escapes. In common with many lizards, they have segmented tails which can easily be broken off through careless handling, and so they must be held lightly around the shoulders and fore-limbs, never by the tail.

There is one fairly common lizard from Europe which I do not recommend for the vivarium. It is a beautiful emerald green creature, the Green Lizard (*Lacerta viridis*). It is not as numerous as it used to be, but can still be seen in parts of the southern countries. There was a very attractive race of these lizards in Jersey, with Cambridge-blue throats, but they were

Top The brilliantly coloured Jewelled Lizard (*Lacerta lepida*) can be found in dry regions of Spain and North Africa.

Above The European Sand Lizard will become a satisfactory inmate of the vivarium if given a reasonable amount of attention.

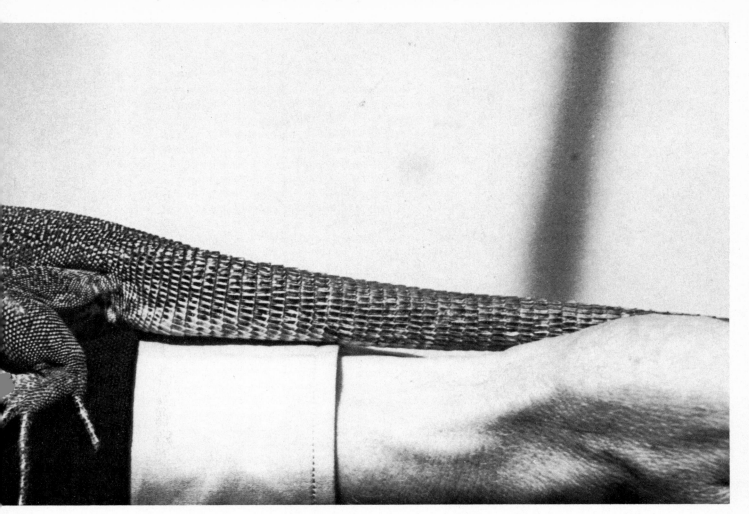

almost hunted out of existence by holiday-makers. Now they are protected and so perhaps they will increase in number once more.

The Green Lizards and many of the tropical reptiles which are difficult to keep in vivariums will often thrive if allowed to live in semi-natural conditions. In temperate countries an outdoor reptiliary is suitable for many of the temperate reptiles to live in all the year round and for some of the tropical ones to live in during the summer months. The position of the enclosure is important. It must be in a warm part of the garden and should not be over-shadowed by trees. It should be on raised ground and have some sort of soak-away or drainage to prevent flooding. The retaining wall may be made of smooth metal or hard plastic sheets, but I personally prefer brick walls plastered over with very smooth cement. Smoothness is necessary to prevent the inmates climbing out. It is wise to arrange an overhang of 6 to 12 inches (15 to 30 centimetres) depending on the size of the animal that is being kept. The ground of the reptiliary should be zoned, with patches of loam, peat, sand and gravel, and small shrubs should be planted to give areas of shade. Pieces of limestone or sandstone rock can be firmly imbedded to look like outcrops and to form a margin to a pool. A cave-like cubicle with an interior, which is easily accessible but still very sheltered, should be

provided. The temperate specimens will hibernate in this cave if it is packed with dry moss and leaves and is frost-proof. An inspection cover is a useful refinement and may consist of a flat stone or metal plate which can be hidden under soil.

The size and shape of the reptiliary is a matter of personal preference, but it should be borne in mind that sharp corners have several disadvantages. It is advisable for it to have smooth outside walls, otherwise it may become a rodent trap. I have known of occasions when a stray rat has taken up residence in an outdoor reptiliary, during the winter, and has killed and eaten the hibernating inmates. In cold parts of the country it is advisable to install a low wattage heater in the cave. A setting of about 10°C to 12°C in winter will prevent frost affecting the residents and a setting of 20° to 22°C in summer will keep them active during any very cold spells.

In the unpredictable climate of temperate countries, the slightly converted greenhouse will make a very satisfactory reptile enclosure and can house a variety of interesting tropical species which will not survive in small vivariums. The greenhouse should have some form of sunblind which can be lowered on the occasions when the sun becomes unbearably hot. It should also have good ventilation, with windows and doors covered in fine metal or nylon gauze. This is not only

a necessary precaution against reptiles escaping, but also prevents the loss of insect food. A high wattage light should be available on dull days and there should be some form of heating which can be arranged to keep zones of the interior of the house hot, allowing the reptiles to choose hot or cool areas. Plants, branches, pools or dishes may be experimented with to discover the best positioning and type, and heaps of leaves, dry soil or sand should be placed in the greenhouse to provide digging and tunnelling facilities.

Some of the most interesting and fascinating lizards that can be kept in a reptile house of this type are the chameleons. Although they are not easy creatures to feed, the trouble involved is well worthwhile. It is fascinating to watch one of these creatures chase a grasshopper across the branches from one end of the house to the other and then, when about 10 inches (25 centimetres) away from its victim, shoot out its long sticky tongue to effect the capture. It makes one feel that all the efforts in the constructing of the house were worthwhile and that the animals are living in very near natural conditions.

One species of chameleon is found in southern Spain and Portugal but it is getting scarcer all the time and one is indeed fortunate to see them in the wild. For really impressive chameleons one must go to East Africa and Madagascar, where there are some of the most curious kinds with one, two, or more horns on their heads and some with sail-like fins running down

Above A striking reptilian pet, an Iguana, is offered a banana.

Right With its slow movements, its weird turretted eyes, its strange method of feeding and its ability to change colour, the chameleon, is a fascinating lizard to keep.

the length of their backs.

The Jackson Chameleon (*Chameleo jacksoni*) is one of the most grotesque lizards. It is 8 to 10 inches (20 to 25 centimetres) long with a ridged back and a large horn above each eye and one on the nose, which gives it a similar appearance to the extinct *Triceratops* of millions of years ago.

Sometimes these lizards can be seen for sale but before being bought they should be examined carefully to ascertain that they are fairly fit. They are wonderful, but difficult, creatures to keep. They often refuse to feed until they have settled down in their new surroundings and, in consequence, they are generally in very poor condition when offered for sale. It is not easy to identify a reptile in poor health but certain conditions should be looked for. For instance, if a lizard or snake has not shed its skin completely, but has pieces of dried skin stuck firmly on parts of its body, it should be ascertained whether or not it has had access to water. If it has had access to water and the skin has still not been shed easily there may be serious reasons for this condition. If breathing is noisy, or there is mucus

Left and above A Jackson's Chameleon catches a locust. Sometimes difficulty is experienced in retracting the long tongue. A regular supply of insect food for the pet chameleon can be ensured by maintaining a locust colony.

around the mouth or nostrils, or the mouth does not close tightly, the animal should be left in the shop. With chameleons I have found that the first sign of serious inanition shows in the eye turrets. A healthy and well-fed specimen has bulging eye sockets, allowing the eyes to swivel around as if on stalks. If the chameleon is in poor condition the eyes sink in and there is little chance of it regaining good health. A pale yellow-coloured body is another indication of poor condition in a chameleon. It normally has a colour range from very pale cream, through green and brown to almost black. These shades change largely due to temperature and, to a lesser degree, the surroundings; but if in reasonably warm conditions it remains a rather sickly yellow, then one can be sure that it is very ill indeed and may soon die.

All lizards are insectivorous except for one group, the iguanas, which are mainly vegetarians, but even they feed on insects when young, and so it is necessary to make certain that the pet lizard can be supplied with sufficient insect food. If one resides in rural areas insect-collecting can be carried out in the spring and summer with the aid of nets which can be used to scoop insects from the long grass. Large pickle jars sunk into the ground and baited with damp bread, fruit or meat will trap an assortment of beetles, and lights placed in barrels with apertures that allow the light to be seen will encourage many flying insects, which can be collected the following morning. Pro-

fessionally made, very efficient moth-traps, utilizing a high wattage bulb, are available. If these are used, the rare species of moths should be released to help conserve the world's rarer insects. The lizards will eat many of the commoner kinds. For town dwellers, and of course during the winter when insects cannot be found, several kinds of insects may be bred or purchased. The most popular insect for feeding animals is probably the Mealworm. This is the larva of the Mealworm Beetle which is widely used for feeding birds and insectivorous animals. They are about the cleanest type of insect, feeding on bran or other farinaceous food, but they thrive when small quantities of grated vegetables, such as carrot, are added to their diet. Since their life cycle spans about one year, a colony should be started well in advance of the time when beetles or larvae are required. A colony can be started in a large biscuit tin, three-quarters full of bran, with pieces of sacking on top and a few beetles placed inside. The temperature should be kept at about 24°C and twice a week a little grated carrot should be placed on top of the sacking.

Blow flies or bluebottles are another useful food for lizards and are easily produced. The larvae of these are the gentles or maggots sold in angling shops. These can be used sparingly as food while others can be placed in a series of bottles, kept at various temperatures to ensure a continuous supply of flies. After a few days the gentles form a chrysalis from which the blow fly emerges. In the summer it is not necessary to buy maggots. A piece of meat or a fish-head, left well away from the house, will become fly-blown, that is, it will become covered with the eggs of blow flies. These will then develop into maggots. However, a very unpleasant smell accompanies the production of maggots and it is perhaps best left to the bait companies, who produce vast quantities every year.

Grasshoppers are the main source of food for lizards in their natural environment. There are more than 5,000 species of these insects around the world and the lizards probably keep down excessive numbers of at least a few kinds.

It is not difficult to collect the smaller kinds during the summer but for a regular supply of insect food, the locust, which is one of the largest grasshoppers, is unsurpassed. They are exceedingly easy to breed in fairly large quantities. They can be used as food from the time of hatching until they become adult insects. Their breeding case should be about 15 inches (38 centimetres) by 15 inches and 24 inches (60 centimetres) high. It needs a glass front and small perforated zinc panels in the side for ventilation. A suitable door should be installed on one side to allow for servicing and feeding. A false bottom of perforated zinc should be arranged about 4 inches (10 centimetres) above the case bottom and should have cut-outs to allow for jars to be placed underneath. The jars are filled with

damp sand made up from five parts of dry sand and one part of water. The inside temperature of the case should be maintained at 28° to 34°C and this can be achieved by suspending a 60 watt electric lamp from the roof of the case. The locusts should be fed on fresh grass each day, any refuse or grass which is uneaten being removed. After the pairing of the adult locusts several egg-pods, each containing up to a hundred eggs, are laid in the jars and these will hatch in about two weeks. Small twigs placed inside the case will assist the locust when shedding its skin periodically during its growth phase. When first hatched the hoppers are very small and are extremely useful as food for very young lizards. In fact, a successful locust colony should always be able to provide insect food in a great variety of sizes.

Earthworms, which are so valuable for the feeding of terrapins and many of the lizards, are easily procured in damp weather if one lives in the country, but otherwise can pose a problem. A regular supply can be assured by starting a 'worm farm' in a cool spot in the corner of the garden or in a shed. One method is to make a pit filled with good loamy soil and leaf mould and to place a quantity of earthworms in it. A little waste vegetable matter should be placed under the first few inches of soil and as this is used up by the worms a fresh supply should replace it. A sprinkling of oatmeal and bran can also be added with advantage. The pit must be kept damp but should not be allowed to flood and in wet weather it will need to be provided with a cover to keep off excess rain.

The alternative method is to have the 'earthworm

Above The small, harmless Grass Snake is an ideal snake to keep as a pet.

Right A pet earns its keep. When its owner was paymaster with a travelling circus, this fine Indian Python was not only kept as a pet but was taken to the wages caravan, where it provided security for its keeper. He was certain that the sight of a large snake would deter any potential wage thieves from furthering their ambitions.

farm' in boxes which can easily be obtained from the local fruiterer. The wooden boxes should be lined with old sacking and filled with loam and leaf mould, and about 5 ounces (125 grammes) of oatmeal. Hessian or old sacking should be draped over the boxes to assist in keeping the contents moist. The oatmeal can be replenished each week.

This 'farm' can be stocked by digging up worms during damp weather, or by the much easier method of purchasing some from the local angling shop or bait company. Usually they are sold in quantities of a pound (0.5 kilogramme), that is about 1,000 worms.

When required, the boxes are emptied out on to a polythene sheet. If several containers are used in rotation the inmates are less disturbed and will breed in sufficient numbers to exceed the pets' requirements, unless the reptile collection is a very large one. In a properly constructed 'wormery' the worms should lay an egg capsule each week or so and each capsule produces about a dozen worms.

So far, in this chapter, I have not mentioned the keeping of snakes. Quite a number of them are kept

privately, outside zoos, and often very successfully, since the private collector is invariably able to give more attention to individuals than is always possible in large zoological collections.

One of the main drawbacks to keeping snakes is the necessity of feeding them on freshly killed animals. There is a world-wide belief that snakes will not eat dead food. This is a fallacy. It is certainly true that in their own domain snakes feed on live animals, but in captivity dead animals will be accepted, especially if a little subterfuge is adopted by the owner when he presents the food. Many snakes related to the Grass Snakes (*Natrix natrix*) frequent marshy areas and feed mainly on frogs. These are not easy to procure for captive snakes, but small fishes may be substituted, and I have on occasions given difficult-to-feed snakes skinned mice, which they have taken as readily as frogs. Such snakes are also very partial to newly-born mice and rats. The small constricting snakes, such as European and American whip snakes (*Coluber* species), Bull Snakes (*Pituophis catenifer*), Pine Snakes (*P. melanoleucus*), young pythons and Boa Constrictors, will always eat dead rats or mice. There is no necessity for worry if a newly obtained snake refuses food for the first week or two. They often take a while to settle down in a vivarium and will not eat in the interval. If it has been ascertained that the temperature is suitable, that is it fluctuates between 24° and 25°C for temperate snakes and between 25° and 30°C for more tropical specimens, and if there is a dish of water large enough to enable the snake to completely submerge itself, then a healthy snake should settle down and feed. When a dead rat or mouse is first offered it should be held by the tail in a long pair of forceps and dangled above the snake's nose. Alternatively it can be placed in front of the reptile's nose and moved about with a stick. One finds that after the first few feeds the sticks or forceps are no longer necessary and the dead animal can simply be placed inside the vivarium.

Very often the pet snake is handled too much before it is offered food, and it then refuses to eat. On no account should it be handled prior to or just after feeding. I have known many small boas and pythons which would feed while being held in the hand, but they are exceptional. It is unwise to handle a snake after it has fed, since, if disturbed, it can regurgitate the meal, which is harmful to the reptile and exceedingly unpleasant to the handler!

The quantity and frequency of feeding is to a certain extent determined by experience. The inexperienced keeper of snakes is usually astounded when his snakes go for weeks or months without feeding, and then suddenly devour several rodents at one sitting, so that their body is distended until the meal is eventually digested. This behaviour is quite normal, and there is no need to worry unduly if a pet snake has not eaten recently, provided that its living conditions are suit-

Left A child with a pet boa. It should always be remembered that a snake should never be handled prior to or just after feeding.

Above The author with his beautiful Royal Python (*Python regius*).

able for it. I have known small Sand Boas (*Eryx johni*) of less than 12 inches (30 centimetres) which did not feed for nine months and Reticulate Pythons (*Python reticulatus*) which refused food for two years. In both these cases, at the end of the time mentioned, the snakes eventually fed and they lived for many years. There is another period when snakes do not feed; it starts about eight or ten days before they shed their skin. At this time the eyes become cloudy for a few days, clearing again a day or two before the actual slough. Having shed the skin the snakes are once again ready to feed. Snakes which are growing quickly may slough every four or five weeks, while more mature specimens do so less frequently. There is just one point to watch for after a snake has shed its skin and that is that it has shed the cusps or films from over its eyes; they should be on the old skin looking like tiny watch glasses. If they are not, they will need to be removed from the snake with the aid of forceps. It is a tricky procedure and on the first occasion it is wise to ask for the assistance of an experienced reptile keeper.

If you are interested in keeping reptiles, remember that even the experts have a great deal to learn about keeping these most fascinating and puzzling creatures.

Highly venomous snakes should not be kept by individuals. They should be left to the care of zoos, which have suitable facilities and which keep stocks of anti-snakebite serum. I have known of several individuals who have kept venomous snakes, with dire consequences to themselves. At the same time they have caused a great deal of unnecessary trouble to police, hospitals, and their own families.

Exploitation

From his primitive beginnings man has exploited animals. This exploitation has been carried so far that it has brought about the disappearance of a great number of species, some of which were numerous even a few years ago. It is generally accepted as being very reasonable for animals to be used as food, to provide clothing, and to serve man in other ways. To increase their usefulness to man special strains of both mammals and birds have been developed from the wild creatures, enabling them to be farmed under conditions which were previously unsuitable. They have been selectively bred to produce more meat, milk, eggs and other commodities. In some cases the stocks now harvested and utilized exceed the numbers which once roamed free. Frequently the domesticated animal is very unlike its wild ancestor.

Often exploitation is carried beyond ethical bounds. Certain reptiles have been ruthlessly treated, some-times so much so that they have become extinct. The giant tortoises provide an example. These great harmless giants had changed very little in size, shape or habits for millions of years. In the Pliocene period, ten to one million years ago, they were numerous all over the world and very fine fossil remains have been discovered in France, Egypt, India and the Americas. Some were larger than the ones we know today; the Indian Atlas Tortoise (*Colossochelys atlas*), the fossil skeleton of which was reconstructed at the British Museum, is estimated to have been nearly 8 feet (2.5 metres) across.

By the Pleistocene era, one million years ago, the giant tortoises had disappeared from the land masses and were only found on groups of volcanic islands. In the Pacific they roamed on the Galapagos group and in the Indian Ocean on three groups, the Seychelles, the Comoros, and the Mascarene Islands.

It is difficult to envisage the huge numbers of tor-

toises which thrived on these volcanic rocks. A visitor to the Seychelles in 1691, François Lequat, wrote: 'land turtles are plentiful sometimes in flocks of three thousand'.

It is understandable that they thrived on these oceanic islands with a pleasantly equable climate, a sufficiency of vegetation and no enemies to interfere with their unhurried life. Darwin describes episodes in their lives in his diary of the voyage of the Beagle. He calculated that they normally walked about 4 miles (6.5 kilometres) each day on the Galapagos Islands, often treading the same well-worn tracts to pools of

Previous page The eggs of the Leatherback Turtle are caught by a Malay as they are laid.

A common sight before protection was given to the giant tortoises of the Galapagos Islands.

rainwater. He used to meet a file of the tortoises on their way, and another file returning. Their whole life was unhurried and orderly. Their courtship was impressive but very simple and slow, but then one would not expect anything different from animals weighing up to 500 pounds (227 kilogrammes) with little short legs!

The group of islands bearing the Spanish name for tortoise, the Galapagos, had a different species of giant tortoise on each island but very few species exist today. They were given the names of the islands upon which they lived and so there were Chatham Island Tortoises, Abingdon Island Tortoises, and very many others.

Dampier, the seventeenth-century explorer, was surprised to find so many tortoises living on the islands. Although from then onwards their numbers were greatly reduced by passing whalers and buccaneers, pleased to be able to collect fresh meat, they were still numerous. Their main decline in numbers commenced when the islands were used by the Ecuador government as penal settlements and the convicts and herds of pigs practically annihilated the fauna and flora of the islands. Even so, up to 1835 most islands had some of the giants roaming around. However, passing ships took away the adult tortoises and their eggs. Some were just cut up and the flesh put into barrels, and the huge heaps of broken shells left behind told the sad story. Although it is too late to save many species, those remaining are now protected, a measure so necessary for their continued existence. Now at last they appear to be safe on the Galapagos Islands.

The tortoises of the Indian Ocean Islands received similar treatment to that which was meted out to the Pacific giants. The Mascarine Islands were the first group to have their stock depleted. In 1759 a shipping service (of four ships) was established solely for transporting the giant tortoises from Rodriguez Island to Mauritius, and in eighteen months 30,000 of these creatures were exported to Mauritius for food. One ship was reported to have carried 6,000 animals, many of which were used to provision naval vessels. Those remaining on the Aldabras and Seychelles are now protected. With scientific assistance and legal protection, the remaining species are building up their meagre numbers, and it is now possible that in the distant future we may yet see 'flocks' browsing upon these islands, as happened 200 or 300 years ago.

One would imagine that a more enlightened world would prevent disasters overtaking other groups of animals in the way they have the giant tortoises, but the great marine turtles are all likely to disappear in the next few years, unless more protection is forthcoming throughout the world's oceans. Many of the breeding grounds where these giants deposit their eggs are being protected to prevent the eggs being removed, and the young turtles are being reared in safe areas. In other parts it is too much to expect undernourished people

94

Above left As a result of the demand for turtle soup the number of Green Turtles in the oceans of the world is dangerously low.

Left Alligator numbers have diminished alarmingly over the last fifty years as a result of their mass slaughter for the skin trade.

Above Young crocodilians like this Mississippi Alligator are killed, stuffed and sold as novelties to tourists.

to forgo the opportunity of making a great deal of money, by capturing the sea creatures which are in such demand. The Hawksbill Turtle (*Eretmochelys imbricata*) was hunted for its shell only. It was the source of the tortoiseshell which was used for adornment, fashionable toilet articles and furniture. When plastics became popular, the demand for genuine tortoiseshell decreased at first, but the respite did not last long. Tortoiseshell articles have once more come into vogue at high prices. Other parts of the body are used for the manufacture of turtle soup. The large Hawksbill, nearly 3 feet (1 metre) long and weighing about 120 pounds (55 kilogrammes) can only provide about 3 pounds (1.5 kilogrammes) of tortoiseshell, and

yet turtle hunters found it profitable work. When it was found that about the same weight of calipee could be taken from the bridging of the top and bottom shell of the turtle and sold at very high prices, the hunting of turtles gathered momentum. Calipee is dried by the turtle catchers and sold for the manufacture of turtle soup, which is often prepared with extracts of other meats.

At one time it was only the Green Turtle (*Chelonia mydas*) which provided turtle soup and the whole turtle was used for this purpose. I have seen warehouses in London where these creatures were kept alive for weeks, with little more attention than a spraying of water from hosepipes, until they were finally despatched for soup. Weeks previously they had floated harmlessly in warm Caribbean seas. These large maritime creatures would probably have ended up in other European or American cities if not in London. I feel that it would have been more justifiable for them to have been eaten by the hungry natives of the areas where they were captured, than to have provided just one course to a prestige meal.

Now the chefs do not require the whole turtle to be transported alive; they are satisfied with the calipee. The turtle will perhaps suffer less by being slaughtered

Above African crocodile hunters with their catch.

Right Crocodile skins hanging out to dry at a Singapore tannery.

when captured, but the demand for calipee is growing and transporting it is much easier than transporting the whole animal, and so, unless protection can be increased, it is very likely that in the immediate future we are going to find that the Hawksbill and the other giant turtles of the ocean have become extinct. The largest of the sea turtles, the Leatherback (*Dermochelys coriacea*), which has been known to weigh up to 1,400 pounds (636 kilogrammes), is perhaps an exception since it is not of great commercial value. In parts of India they were eaten in curries and the oil extracted from them was used to preserve boats, but their breeding grounds are now vigilantly protected in Trengganu, Malaysia, and in other places in South East Asia.

The Green Turtle is also receiving a tremendous amount of help to survive. The government of Costa Rica, which up till 1957 had derived some income from the turtle hunters, very generously gave protection to the breeding grounds along its coastline. In addition, many charitably-minded organizations are working towards re-stocking the American waters in the regions where the turtles were once prolific.

Like the great turtles, the crocodilians have changed very little in appearance over the millions of years, but in numbers they have diminished alarmingly, especially over the last fifty years. It is almost a certainty that the American Alligator (*Alligator mississippiensis*) would now be extinct if the government protection laws had not been instigated in 1944 to prevent their wholesale slaughter. The records of the sales of their skins on the

American markets made a very grim picture when we find that in 1929 some 190,000 were sold; in 1938 there were 80,000 offered for sale and the year before they were legally protected, the hunters were unable to collect more than 6,000 in Florida. Even now poaching occurs in the national parks.

The crocodiles of Africa, Asia, Australia and South America are being depleted even more than the alligators. As a result of the high prices that crocodile skin is commanding, the hunting of these animals is being carried out more ruthlessly than ever before, using high-velocity guns, speed-boats and modern trapping methods. Again in some of the great national parks, where protection has been given to these reptiles, it is nearly impossible with the present resources allowed for upkeep to prevent poaching and it is reported that one can travel hundreds of miles along tropical rivers without seeing one crocodile. A few years ago there were thousands.

It is not only the large specimens which are killed. The very young crocodilians are collected soon after hatching, skinned and made into novelties for the tourist trade. Happily, this trade seems to be declining, largely due to the advent of plastic imitations, which are equal in appearance to a real baby croc, and quite as

Below As a result of the demand for crocodile skin, these creatures are often collected in vast numbers and kept in appallingly cramped conditions until they are slaughtered.

Right A slaughtered crocodile is skinned.

suitable for dangling from the rear window of a car.

The terrapins which frequent fresh or brackish waters have always been a source of food for the local people. When H. W. Bates visited the Amazon in 1862, he reported that forty-eight million eggs were collected each year from the nesting sites of the Great River Turtle (*Podecnemis expansa*). He does not state how many of the adult terrapins were eaten; but it is no small wonder that this species is one for which the animal conservationists report the need of special protection if it is to be saved from extinction.

Terrapins have always been a popular food in North America and the Diamond-back Terrapin (*Malaclemys terrapin*) was at one period elevated to the level of caviar by the connoisseurs. Nowadays many other kinds find their way to restaurants, especially the Snapping Turtle (*Chelydra serpentina*). This terrapin is an ugly creature with a large head, heavily-clawed feet and a long thick tail with sawlike spines along the top. It can inflict a nasty bite, but the power of the jaws is often exaggerated and even the largest specimens cannot sever the feet of bathers as has been commonly stated. Sometimes these turtles are fattened before being eaten, and at one time they were placed in large swill bins to feed on kitchen waste. After several months, they would have increased their weight more than twofold.

Snakes are not eaten in Europe today, except perhaps for the few tins of rattlesnake meat which are sent over as 'gimmicky' specialities. Many years ago in France some country people ate certain of the more common European snakes. In old references the Grass Snake (*Natrix natrix*), the Aesculapian Snake (*Elaphe longissima*) and the Adder (*Vipera berus*) were known

Left At one time the flesh of the Diamond-back Terrapin was considered as much of a delicacy as caviar.

Below Snapping Turtle dishes are often found on restaurant menus in North America.

Above Rat snakes are among the various snakes eaten by the Chinese.

Right The shell of the large Hawksbill Turtle provides the tortoiseshell of commerce.

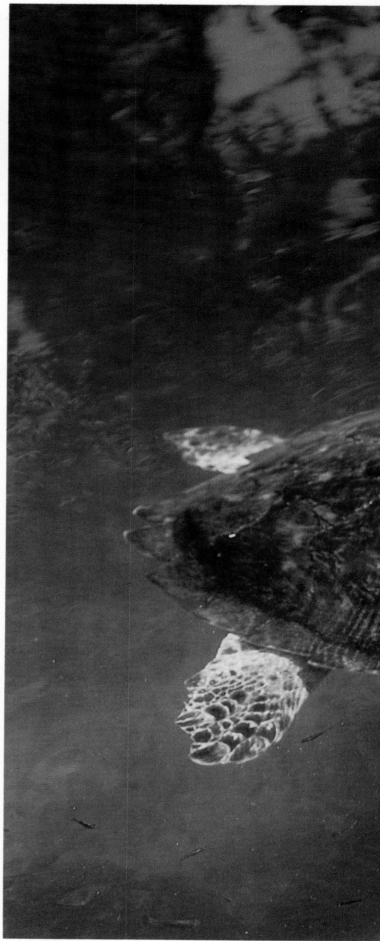

as Hedge, Bush and Mountain Eels respectively. The Adder was also used in the preparation of medicines.

In Asian countries many species are eaten and now the larger pythons, which were quite numerous, are being hunted ruthlessly. A few years ago, the price of python meat reached phenomenal heights in Malaysia and this, coupled with the high returns received for the skin, made it more profitable to supply meat and skin dealers with dead specimens than zoological gardens with live specimens. However, sometimes live pythons were caught and exhibited in food shops specializing in snake flesh, until sufficient orders were received to make it economic to kill and apportion the carcass to customers who had reserved their particular section of snake!

In China and Japan many small snakes are eaten, including some of the most venomous sea snakes. In Hong Kong, boxes containing a variety of snakes can be seen outside restaurants which specialize in snake dishes. Cobras, kraits (*Bungarus* species), rat snakes (*Elaphe* species) and Moon Snakes (*Lunelaps christieanus*) are all heaped together, looking like the heaps of live eels which were often to be seen in boxes outside London's jellied-eel shops years ago. When I sampled some of the very highly recommended snake dishes, I found them rather insipid, except where very pungent flavouring had been used to lace the liquid. However, I did eventually become a good customer; I purchased a number of live specimens, which the proprietor imagined I was going to cook at home, but which were actually destined for exhibition at the London Zoo. Although some of the same species were still to be found on Hong Kong Island these snakes had been imported from the Chinese mainland. To prevent accidents during transit each snake had

had its mouth sewn up very neatly. It certainly enabled the kitchen staff to handle venomous snakes quite safely, but I found the removal of the stitches quite a tedious chore. I like to think that the cobras did at least appreciate the freedom to yawn once more. One of them became remarkably tame and lived many years at Regents Park. A large Banded Krait (*Bungarus fasciatus*), a yellow and black-banded snake, was not so grateful. Within a couple of hours of having his mouth unstitched he had eaten two of his smaller companions. I should have remembered that the Banded Kraits are cannibals. Perhaps that was another reason why it had had its mouth sewn up!

On special feast days in China several species of snakes are served at banquets. On one such occasion, the Tiger and Dragon Feast, a combination of cat and snake is the main course. Some of the snakes used for these feasts are imported from India. Not only do snakes provide meat and an ingredient for soups, but some are used in the preparation of a medicinal wine. In China the gall bladders are always removed before cooking because they are considered to be a very efficient stimulant when swallowed raw, and are in

great demand. In Hainan Island the poisonous sea snakes which drift along the coast are made into a 'snake sausage'.

The Aborigines of Australia will only eat harmless snakes which they always cook, complete with skin, over open fires. The large Carpet Python (*Morelia argus*), which is sometimes more than 10 feet (3 metres) long and the North Queensland Python (*Liasis amethystinus*), which may grow twice as long, are not even chopped up for cooking, but are coiled up like hose-pipes, while snakes of smaller dimensions are rolled in clay and baked.

The depletion of many kinds of reptiles have been brought about because their skins can be used as

Below The large Carpet Python is eaten by the Australian Aborigines. It is not chopped up, but simply coiled like a hosepipe and cooked over an open fire.

Right The Elephant Trunk Water Snake's skin is known as Karung in the skin trade.

Below right A shoe manufactured from cobra skin.

Below left The most dangerous time for the Green Turtle is when it comes ashore to lay its eggs.

Below Malays probing in the sand for the Leatherback Turtle's eggs.

attractive leathers. In addition to the crocodiles and alligators mentioned earlier, many species of snakes and lizards, even some small specimens, are hunted for their skins, and the British Board of Trade figures giving the numbers of skins imported from all over the world make disturbing reading for the naturalist. Very rare species of reptiles living in a rather inaccessible district are suddenly discovered by a native aware of their marketable skin value, and in a short time they are killed, skinned and sun-dried ready for shipping.

I was shocked some years ago when I visited a reptile-skin warehouse in London's dockland and saw heaps of skins bearing trade names based on the skin pattern or country of origin. There were thousands of skins of the Elephant Trunk Water Snake (*Acrochordus javanicus*), known as Karung to the skin trade, the Boa Constrictor and pythons. Even the skin of the large Iguana (*Iguana iguana*) of South and Central America had become chameleon-skin to the dealers! There were bales of skins of a banded snake which at first I did not recognize, especially under the trade name of Ermaline, but I later found that it was the little Dog-faced Water Snake (*Cerberus rhynchops*), which lives in the muddy streams and ditches of Malaysia. I was informed that they are only useful for trimmings and belts! The very large lizards were certainly well represented; there were Nile Monitors (*Varanus niloticus*), and White-throated Monitors (*V. albigularis*) from Africa and Great Water Lizards (*V. salvator*) from South East Asia. There were even imported skins of the less well-known Alligator Lizard (*Dracaena guianensis*), a striking nut-brown lizard which feeds only on crustaceans and is only rarely seen in zoo reptile collections. I knew the reason when I saw the numbers of skins.

It is a pity that the general public will not accept synthetic reptile skins. The plastics industries have produced wonderfully realistic material, with correct colouring, patterning and scalation. Even the reptile expert has difficulty in distinguishing a genuine skin from a fake. I have been assured that the better quality imitation skin wears equally as well as the real thing. But there is always someone who will demand the real snake, lizard or crocodile skin.

Whether or not one really approves of reptiles being used in exhibitions of charming or dancing, at least they are not being slaughtered in their hundreds as they are for the skin trade. Snake charming, in which cobras and flutes are used, is not often seen away from Egypt or India, but snake dancing, which is just a display using harmless snakes, is seen in night-clubs all around the world. The usually attractive girl dancer, wearing oriental apparel, allows the snake to glide around her body while she moves in time with the music. There are some aspects which ought to be dropped from these displays, such as swinging the snake around by the tail, gradually lowering it to the

Left This male model's outfit is made from python skin. So often the fashion world undermines the work of conservationists.

Above An enormous Anaconda skin, which is destined for manufacture into ladies' shoes, is proudly displayed in a warehouse.

ground. It is reported that after several years of this treatment, one python had to have part of its tail amputated.

The Indian Python (*Python molurus*) is the most popular snake for snake dancing, although the Boa Constrictor and other large snakes are often used.

Considering the way that they are handled and the fact that they are housed in stage property baskets, kept warm with protected electric light bulbs and transported to clubs inside suitcases, it is surprising that many live several years. It is necessary that more than one snake be kept if the 'show is always to go on'. It is not advisable to handle a snake which has recently eaten. A few day's rest between meals is necessary, and also it is unwise to handle them just before they shed their skin. Even the most docile snake may become cantankerous at this time. Quite a number of dancers have been bitten through using a snake which was indisposed, or 'sloughing'.

Snake shows seem to fascinate an audience whether they involve dancing, charming or are a part of a film. Just an inset in a jungle film of a snake dropping from a tree in a most unreal manner, or a rattlesnake in a typical studio setting in a cowboy film lends impact and often livens up the otherwise dull sequences. The thrill is, however, only felt by the film-goer who does not see what actually occurred in obtaining the shot. He probably thinks that specially trained snakes are used, but of course there is no such snake.

I have assisted with reptiles in films on several occasions, and actually ended up as the snake charmer complete with cobras and flute in that epic film 'The Land of the Pharoahs'. The difficulties encountered in producing films about animals result from the fact that the directors are not naturalists and expect the animals to do near-impossible feats in front of the cameras. It is a knowledge of their normal behaviour which has to be exploited to obtain the desired result.

Left Snake charming is less harmful to the world's snake population than most aspects of man's exploitation of these creatures. At least it does not require the snake's death as does the trade in skins, for example.

Below The skin of the Iguana is sometimes referred to by dealers as chameleon-skin.

Above A Puff Adder being 'milked'. The acquisition of snake venom for the production of anti-venins and drugs is one aspect of the exploitation of reptiles which can whole-heartedly be condoned.

Right. This dancer enhances her act with snakes from four different countries.

The finest example of depicting reptiles as they really are in films was achieved in the Walt Disney production, 'The Living Desert'.

There are still to be seen, in some fairgrounds, side-shows housing 'a jungle girl and her reptile friends'. The 'jungle girl' sits in a glass-fronted booth and has snakes and lizards either draped around her neck or dangling from a branch. The variety of reptiles is often interesting and in some of these shows I have seen reptiles from six different countries. These displays are not edifying; the girl looks bored and the reptiles are mishandled and badly looked after. The fairground side-shows are usually seasonal, commencing at Easter and closing down at the end of the summer, when the commoner reptiles are disposed of to be re-placed the following year. However, it is becoming increasingly costly to obtain suitable 'stock' and so attempts are made to keep the reptiles alive for as long as possible, often in unsuitable accommodation.

There is at least one facet of the exploitation of reptiles which I feel we must condone and that is their use in the production of anti-venin to counteract bites of venomous snakes. This is prepared by obtaining venom from specific snakes and injecting small quantities of it into horses. The resultant serum is taken from the horse. The snakes are 'milked' of their venom by allowing them to bite over small dishes which collect the liquid. Often it is necessary to massage the poison gland at the same time, to increase the flow of venom; this requires a degree of skill by the technician. Venoms are usually clear, sticky liquids of a pale amber colour. The venom from one snake can produce many phials of anti-venin, but even if this is kept cool its effective life is usually not more than two years, and so the stocks need replenishing regularly, despite their not being used. A great amount of research has taken place in the large serum institutes and pharmaceutical laboratories and now polyvalents are available for various groups of snakes, where previously it was necessary to have a specific serum for each type of snake. There were several pioneering institutions around the world which brought anti-venins to the near perfection that they are today. Three which especially deserve to be mentioned for their contributions to saving the lives of snakebite victims are the Pasteur Institute of Europe, the Haff-gine Institute of India and the Brazilian Serum Institute of Butantan in South America. The last mentioned were preparing anti-venin for the most dreaded of South American snakes, the Fer-de-lance Viper (*Bothrops atrox*) as long ago as 1902. When their own supply of these snakes, from which they extracted the venom, became depleted, they advertised for more live specimens from outlying districts and in a very short time received no less than 7,293!

It is not only for the production of anti-venin that snake venom is of value. The medical profession has discovered several other uses for it in the treatment of diseases. For instance, up until the early 1930's, it was almost impossible to operate successfully on a haemophiliac. Working upon the knowledge that one of the constituents of the venom of the Russell's Viper (*Vipera russelli*) was a coagulant, a Dr Macfarline produced a preparation from it which is used today to prevent excessive bleeding. During the early experimental work I milked great numbers of Russell's Vipers, which were imported from Calcutta. It was a rather tedious task but well worth all the trouble involved. In contrast, venom from other snakes, notably the Malaysian pit-vipers, is used to prevent clotting in certain blood disorders. Even the diluted venom from the Indian Cobra (*Naja naja*) has been used with success in alleviating pain. Perhaps in the future these maligned animals will provide even greater aids to human health.

Survival

In the course of evolution some species of animal die out and are replaced by other species. Certain animals gradually decrease in number, while others, able to adapt to changing conditions, increase in number. Changes in shape and size and development of new species take millions of years. When man first came upon the scene and exploited the animals for his own purpose his depredations were insignificant, being absorbed into the natural pattern of birth and death within an animal population. A little more than a hundred years ago a different picture began to emerge. Modern methods of slaughter were evolving and large commercial undertakings had begun to make use of the animal population of the world without consideration for its future. As a result, certain species were depleted to the point of extinction. Some scientists and people dedicated to animal welfare became concerned, but often their voices were unheard by those with vested interests in animal exploitation. 'Upsetting the balance of nature' was a frequent cry, but a large pro-portion of the general public throughout the world acted like the proverbial Ostrich. Eventually, with influential people taking the lead, conservation measures were discussed.

An early and dramatic enactment of conservation procedure took place in America in 1888, when it became fairly obvious to some far-sighted people that, unless a halt were forthcoming in the ruthless slaughter of the Bison, they would completely disappear from the prairies. At one time it had been estimated that there were fifty million, and yet when a count was made in 1889, their numbers had dwindled to a mere 540. There would have been a slight excuse if they had been made full use of as food, but millions of them were killed only for their hides and to a lesser extent for their tongues, which were regarded as a delicacy. Their bodies were just left to rot.

The Bison Society of America was only just formed in time. It was able to enlist the help of the government and various influential bodies to save the remaining

animals. These were used to form the nuclei of small herds which were successfully established, and in a few years it was announced that their future was secure.

At about the same time in South Africa, President Kruger realised that the animal life of Africa was in jeopardy from the advancement of civilization and that, unless his government acted swiftly, many animals would face complete extermination. He had several opponents, but eventually he won them over to his point of view and it was decided to make a large parcel of land, already rich in animal life, a sanctuary where

Previous page The giant tortoises of the Galapagos Islands appear to have a very good chance of surviving at the present time, but quite a number of problems still require to be solved.

The Nile Crocodile has disappeared from most of Africa as a result of the demand for its skin, but successful conservation schemes are in progress in South Africa.

no hunting could take place. This area, many square miles between the two great rivers, the Sabi and the Crocodile, was the first ever game reserve and was later, in 1926, inaugurated as the now famous Kruger National Park. Many other game reserves have since been modelled on this park.

In Britain the first of the societies established for the conservation of animals was the Society for the Preservation of Wild Fauna of the Empire, which was founded in 1903. The title was later abbreviated to the Fauna Preservation Society. Over the years it has carried out a tremendous amount of valuable work in the conservation field, and it was instrumental in furthering the cause during the thirties especially, when many countries were considering setting up similar societies. After the last war it was realized that for conservation to be completely successful, it must have the backing of all governments throughout the world; and in 1948 The International Union for the Conservation of Nature was formed. The World Wildlife Fund was later created to provide grants which would help to pay the costs of the Union's numerous worthwhile operations.

Conservation is a complex subject and the magnitude of the task is difficult to envisage. I once heard a very fine speaker on the subject state that conservation was 'not just a case of dicky birds and daisies'. How right he was. For example, certain animals may be approaching extinction because thay have become the main source of food for the local people. To combat this, help in providing alternative food would need to be given. Recently two tribes, the Yorouba and the Hanoussa, have moved into Togo territory. These people feed largely on the crocodile, which is not protected in Togo, and so in a short time it is possible that it could be exterminated from this area, as it has been already in most parts of Africa. Often commercial undertakings, which exploit the animals of a region and employ a large amount of local labour, clash with the conservationists. A means of satisfying both camps needs to be devised.

The ranching of an area with domestic animal breeds often harms the indigenous animal population. More research needs to be conducted if domestic and wild animals are to live together in harmony. Potent pesticides have created tremendous havoc when they have been used indiscriminately. All these problems have to be appraised and a practical answer found. For many of the reptiles, the game reserves are likely to be the only salvation, and even here many are in a very precarious position. The Nile Crocodile (*Crocodylus niloticus*) has already disappeared from most of Africa as a result of the demand for its skin, but successful conservation schemes are in action in South Africa. In the Muzuki Game Park their eggs are being collected and the young crocodiles, when hatched, are being distributed to selected unpopulated areas. In

Ceylon the Estuarine Crocodile (*Crocodylus porosus*) has been given complete protection and in western Australia the same species is protected from hunting for a ten year period which started in 1970. It is hoped that it will recover from the massive exploitation which has taken place. To conserve the New Guinea Crocodile (*Crocodylus novaeguineae*) the Administration of the Territory has made it illegal to deal in skins of a width less than 20 inches (50 centimetres). This should certainly help to protect this interesting animal from extinction. Unfortunately, carrying out these measures is becoming more and more expensive and more and more difficult, since professional poachers are adopting increasingly effective methods of capture. This state of affairs was highlighted in 1968 in Florida. It was then estimated that the numbers of alligators in the state had decreased by ninety-eight per cent in eight years, as a result of the energies of the poachers, who were reckoned to be between 1,000 and 2,000 strong. The American Crocodile (*Crocodylus acutus*) has already become very rare in the United States and, although it is officially protected in Mexico, it is reported by the Conservancy Union that the law is poorly enforced in this country. It is rigorously protected in the Everglades National Park, Florida, and so there is a very good chance that it will remain with us well into the future, in one part of the world at least.

The giant tortoises of the Aldabra Islands, in the Indian Ocean, and the Galapagos Islands, in the Pacific, appear to have a very good chance of surviving at the present time, but quite a number of problems still require to be solved. The Government of Ecuador wisely declared the Galapagos Islands a Sanctuary Area and imposed laws to protect the fauna, but in augmenting these it ran into many difficulties. Some of the islands were being farmed fairly intensively and the indigenous animals were an incumbrance to the farmers. In addition, the giant tortoises were useful 'perks' to local and visiting fishermen. It was in 1959 that a group of far-sighted people set up the Charles Darwin Foundation, with the blessing of the Government, to attempt to preserve for all time the unique animals of the islands. They were agreeably surprised to find, on some of the small islands, 'pockets' of some species of tortoises which had previously been considered extinct. However, their continued existence was threatened by the herds of wild pigs and goats, which had originated from domestic stock. These animals not only destroyed the vegetation but also ate the eggs and young of the tortoises and the unique Marine Iguanas (*Amblyrhynchus cristatus*). A research establishment has been set up on one of the islands, complete with its own reserve, and measures have been taken to reduce the number of feral animals. These have met with some success, but much more still requires to be accomplished before the Foundation will be able to announce that the 'Giants of Galapagos' are safe from extinction.

On the Indian Ocean's group of islands the future of the tortoises is slightly less secure. It has recently been discovered that, although they have disappeared from some of the islands where they were once numerous, there are still very large numbers of them on at least three of the islands of the Aldabra group, and there are very few predatory animals to threaten their

To conserve the New Guinea Crocodile the Administration of the Territory has made it illegal to deal in small skins.

Above The existence of the Charles Darwin Foundation in the Galapagos Islands should ensure the survival of the Marine Iguana.

Left Man's insatiable demand for its shell has placed the Hawksbill Turtle in acute danger of extinction.

existence. But they have one very great disadvantage. They have no great protective body working entirely on their behalf in the way that the Darwin Foundation of the Galapagos does. If their future is to be assured, they must have complete protection, or one day the threatened air base may destroy their island home.

What will eventually become of the giant marine turtles? Some species have received help to survive as mentioned in a previous chapter. Without this dedicated work there would, without doubt, be fewer turtles in the oceans today, but with man's insatiable demand for their flesh, and in the case of the Hawksbill, their shell, they may become extinct in the near future. The reason that the future of these turtles is so grim is not so much that they are slaughtered in large numbers as that their eggs are taken.

It is not only the large reptiles that are disappearing at an alarming rate. Many of the smaller species are becoming rare, or will do so, unless means can be devised to save them. Even reptiles which were previously very common, such as the little Greek Tortoise, are now rapidly disappearing. This is not at all surprising when one learns that Morocco alone has, each year since 1953, exported 100 tons of Greek Tortoises, with an estimated 3,000 to the ton. There are other nauseating records: for the period 1965 to 1967, 750,000 tortoises were exported and about 10,000 killed, so that their shells could be made into banjos for the tourist trade. Now a restriction has been placed on the numbers for export. The latest annual export figures are about 40,000. The British pet dealers have voluntarily agreed to only accept Greek and Herman's Tortoises which have a shell length of 4 inches (10 centimetres) or more. This gesture will go some way to preventing the smaller ones being collected for the pet trade.

Today, the hazards facing the smaller lizards and snakes are such that many species will be threatened with extinction very soon. Motorways take a tremendous toll. It has been reported that 2,000 reptiles have been killed on the roads of just one State of America in a single day. Whether it is the reptile's intention to cross the road or just to sunbathe on the smooth warm surface is irrelevant; once they stray on to the roads their chance of survival is slight. Another devastating blow is dealt to the population of small reptiles by the systematic war waged upon insects by agricultural concerns. Both harmful and harmless insects are destroyed by toxic sprays which thus also affect the small reptiles, either directly, or indirectly by depriving them of their normal insect food. For the majority of reptiles the nature reserves are their only salvation. It is imperative that more are created, especially with the preservation of small animals in mind. Unfortunately, conservation is very costly. Each large game park can only support a certain number of animals. When this limit is exceeded culling has to take place, and any money gained from this can be used to offset at least part of the heavy maintenance costs of the park. I cannot see any reason why large reptiles, pythons and crocodiles for example, should not be 'farmed' in suitable areas, and the surplus be used to defray the expense of protecting smaller reptiles from extinction.

Small reptiles such as the Green Lizard face many hazards today. Motorways and insecticides, for example, take a heavy toll.

One valuable form of conservation that we have not yet mentioned is that carried out by the scientifically orientated zoos. In the very early days of zoos, numbers of rare animals were acquired only to be exhibited to a gaping general public. Often their future was not considered and little effort was made to get them to breed. To some extent a few of the small, badly run establishments still exploit animals in this manner, but generally zoos today are developing a completely new approach to all the intricacies associated with the keeping of wild animals in captivity. It is now considered by zoo managements that it is not ethical, practical, or desirable to keep single, rare animals, if breeding colonies can be established. The exchange or loan of rare animals by one zoo to another, with a view to breeding, is becoming commonplace, and these amicable arrangements, often at international level, have resulted in a great many animals being saved from extinction. This co-operation, which includes the sharing of results of animal research, has enabled rare animals to be bred, when previously they had been considered extremely difficult just to keep in captivity for a short spell. In illustration of this point, one can observe nowadays breeding colonies of the large anthropoid apes, the Chimpanzee, the Orang-Utan and the Gorilla, thriving in the great zoos. It is now certain that in the foreseeable future these animals and many other rare creatures will be able to be reared in sufficient numbers in zoos. The capture of wild stock will perhaps only be necessary for improving the strain.

The breeding of reptiles in the zoos has not been as spectacular as that of the mammals and birds but there have been some notable successes. About twelve years ago, at the San Diego zoo, for instance, giant tortoises (*Testudo elephantopus*) were bred for the first time in any zoo. Specimens of these creatures had been exhibited in many zoos, and, although they had been observed to mate, few fertile eggs had been laid in captivity up until that time. In an Indonesian Zoo, eggs have been laid by Komodo Dragons, but so far no hatching has taken place. However, when more research has been conducted it is almost certain that these rare animals and many others will be able to be bred in captivity.

The zoo's obligation to conservation does not just lie in the breeding of rare animals for exhibition. The modern zoo can be likened to a gigantic ice-berg. The general public sees only the tip, the animal collection, which requires for its maintenance a great deal of thought and energy from a dedicated staff. They do not see the largest part of the ice-berg, the administration offices, the numerous research laboratories, the veterinary and pathology departments, the libraries, the education division, and various other departments, all working to improve the welfare of wild animals in captivity. The resultant findings and recommendations are made freely available to all those bodies which have the welfare of wild animals at heart; and they are of real value when utilized for conservation.

The modern reptile house is a grand shop window designed to display many species, but very few include facilities that would enable breeding colonies to be established. Breeding does take place, but it is mainly incidental. The longevity records for zoo reptiles are impressive and clearly show that the depletion of reptiles in the wild is in no way connected with zoo demands. It is a great credit to the zoo staff that so many of the inmates of reptile houses do live to advanced ages. Examination of zoo reptile records reveals some interesting highlights. We find, for example, that the Cairo Zoo has giant tortoises which have roamed their enclosures for nearly seventy years, and crocodiles which have spent forty years in captivity. Even Greek Tortoises have been there for sixty years. A Chinese Alligator (*Alligator sinensis*) and two Indian Gavials (*Gavialis gangeticus*) lived at the London Zoo for thirty years, and an adult Mississippi Alligator purchased from a circus, lived a further forty-three years there. The famous Swiss Zoo at Basle holds the record for the giant South American water snake, the Anaconda. A specimen was kept there for nearly thirty-two years. As previously mentioned, the record of reptile breeding in zoos is not outstanding, but it is improving all the time as fresh techniques are developed. It is to be hoped that one day visitors will be able to see breeding colonies of reptiles in the zoos, instead of so many individual specimens.

In this book I have attempted to give a general account of those features of reptiles which I consider to be of the greatest interest. It has not been possible to explore in full depth all the fascinating aspects of these creatures. Indeed some subjects, which would perhaps have merited a chapter to themselves had space permitted, have in fact had to be omitted. There is, for instance, the harmless little Malay Flying Snake (*Chrysopelea ornata*) which can glide from high trees; or there are the sea snakes, about which very little is yet known.

Reptiles form a varied and intriguing group of animals. However, for reasons which are sometimes obscure and often quite unfounded, certain members of this class are among the most maligned creatures alive. It is my hope that this book will stimulate an interest in reptiles and by providing information on their true nature will encourage the development of a more amiable attitude to them.

Zoos and animal parks play an important role in the saving of rare animals from extinction. Here an employee of the well-known Port Elizabeth Snake Park poses for the camera with some of his charges. It should be pointed out that it is dangerous for the non-professional snake-keeper to carry venomous snakes in the way shown here.

Acknowledgements

Colour Ardea—D. Burgess 18 (top), 58 (bottom), Ardea—A. Hayward 22, 23, 26; Associated Freelance Artists Ltd.—G. Kinns 18 (bottom); Barnaby's Picture Library 110–111; Bruce Coleman Ltd.—J. Brownlie 30–31, Bruce Coleman Ltd.—J. Burton 50, 51, 54 (bottom), 66, 78, 79, 107, Bruce Coleman Ltd.—B. Coleman 54 (top), Bruce Coleman Ltd.—J. Dermid 58 (top), 70–71, Bruce Coleman Ltd.—D. Hughes 59, 102–103, back jacket, Bruce Coleman Ltd.—P. Jackson front jacket, Bruce Coleman Ltd.—H. Silvester 75; J. Markham 19, 27, 67; Picturepoint Ltd. 99; Syndication International 98; Z.F.A. 106; Zoological Society of London 55, 63, 74.

Black and white Ardea—P. J. Green 28, Ardea—A. Hayward 24 (top), Ardea Photographics 109; Barnaby's Picture Library 2–3, 69; Biofotos 53 (bottom) 83; British Museum (Natural History) 20–21, 24 (bottom), 25 (top), 25 (bottom); Camerapix—Mohamed Amin 15, 39, 46; Camera Press Ltd. 16; J. Allan Cash 37, 123; Bruce Coleman Ltd.—S. C. Bisserot 6–7, 68 (bottom), 77, 111, Bruce Coleman Ltd.—J. R. Brownlie 44, 104, Bruce Coleman Ltd.—J. Burton 47, 53 (top), 116–117, Bruce Coleman Ltd.—R. Bustard 48–49, 72–73, Bruce Coleman Ltd.—J. Dermid 64, Bruce Coleman Ltd.—S. Gillsater 29, 34, Bruce Coleman Ltd.—C. A. W. Guggisberg 12–13, Bruce Coleman Ltd.—D. Hughes 112, Bruce Coleman Ltd.—R. Kinne 32–33, 38 (bottom), 80 (bottom), 94 (top), 94 (bottom), 100, Bruce Coleman Ltd.—L. Lee Rue 101, Bruce Coleman Ltd.—H. W. Silvester 114–115, Bruce Coleman Ltd.—M. W. F. Tweedie 41, 90–91, Bruce Coleman Ltd.—H. E. Uible 88, Bruce Coleman Ltd.—J. Wallis 42–43; Fox Photos Ltd. 82; Hamlyn Group—Prague Museum 9, Hamlyn Group—Bruno del Priore 8; Keystone Press Agency Ltd.—60–61, 87, 105 (bottom), 113; J. Markham 10–11, 14, 76, 80–81, 86, 120–121; Picturepoint Ltd. 97; Popperfoto 65, 95, 96 (left), 96 (right), 108; W. Suschitzky 52 (bottom), 56–57; A. Taylor 68 (top), 89; World Wildlife Fund 92–93, 119 (top); Zoological Society of London 36, 38 (top), 52 (top), 84, 85, 102, 105 (top), 118, 119 (bottom).

Index

Index